www.thefeastpress.com

The Feast: Re-Forming Ignatian Spirituality

THE FEAST

Re-Forming Ignatian Spirituality

by Joseph F. Duggan

Published by THE FEAST PRESS
www.thefeastpress.com
info@thefeastpress.com

Design by Melody Stanford

Cover artwork by Marilyn Collins, "Free The Form," acrylic on canvas

ISBN 10: 0997013605
ISBN 13: 978-0-9970136-0-3

First edition

Printed in the United States of America

DEDICATION

The Feast: Re-Forming Ignatian Spirituality is in your hands due to the constant encouragement, loving support, and creativity of my beloved partner, Stefani Schatz. My life with Stefani is rooted in feast. After hearing my spiritual journey for over a decade, Stefani said to me, "One day you really must write a book." Stefani made the suggestion and invitation several times before I started to write. Stefani continued to play a key role, listening to every word I wrote, and even suggested the change of my original word "reformed" to "re-forming."

CONTENTS

PART I: "Free The Form" a Meditation on Re-forming

Free the Form

PART II: The Autobiography of Ignatius as a Spiritual Autobiographical Exercise

Appendix: The Feast Resources and Some Spiritual Exercises

PREFACE

The Feast: Re-Forming Ignatian Spirituality has been written both for those who are familiar with *The Spiritual Exercises of Ignatius of Loyola* and *A Pilgrim's Journey: The Autobiography of St. Ignatius of Loyola*, and for those who are curious about life in relation with God in mission. I have known people who wanted to do a thirty-day Ignatian retreat, but, for a variety of reasons, *The Spiritual Exercises* didn't work for them the way they were originally formulated.

My goal in writing this is for you, the reader, to have the freedom and the tools to take Ignatius' wisdom but adapt it to your own needs. There are many ways to read and use this book. If you have never heard of Ignatius of Loyola or have never experienced spiritual direction or a retreat, the Annotated Bibliography contains resources on all these topics, which might add to your appreciation of this book. Alternatively, you might read Parts I and V and hear the accounts of three women who experienced a long retreat I designed called "The Feast," based on Ignatius' works. You decide.

This book begins its exploration of Ignatius with his *Autobiography*, not his *Spiritual Exercises*. By starting with the *Autobiography* I wanted to return to the beginning of Ignatius of Loyola's spiritual journey when as a new convert, his primary teacher was the Holy Spirit. Although Ignatius in *The Spiritual Exercises* continues to rely on the Holy Spirit, the indoctrination of Jesuits and other retreatants through the *Exercises* begins to take a turn towards surrender and submission to the hierarchical church and the central authority of the superior rather than the Holy Spirit. As a former Jesuit, I wanted to retain the rich spiritual wisdom of Ignatius while, at the same time, accommodating the way my spiritual needs changed after I left the

Society of Jesus. As I make this shift I want to emphasize and prioritize the primacy of the Holy Spirit rather than the authority of a religious superior as modeled in the Society of Jesus. It is commonly said in the Society of Jesus that the relationship between the superior and subject is that: you (subject) discern, I (superior) discern, he (the superior) decides!

The majority of books on *The Spiritual Exercises* have not been adapted for the spiritual needs of those who are not called to be Jesuits. While some translations of *The Spiritual Exercises* use more contemporary language, the pre-modern Roman Catholic theology of *The Spiritual Exercises* has not been challenged in ways that allow it to speak to the twenty-first century spiritual seeker. In the pages ahead I will show, through my spiritual autobiography, why I, a protestant Episcopal priest, feel it necessary to shift the traditional Ignatian emphasis from penitential, submissive obedience to feast and a continuous process of re-forming.

Following Ignatius' vision of seeing God everywhere, in every aspect of life, feasting occurs every day. With this alternative reading lens, I decouple Ignatian spiritual wisdom from the rigid boundaries of Ignatius' *Spiritual Exercises* and the pre-reformed traditions of exclusively Jesuit trained spiritual directors. I invite readers to radically follow the life and actions of Jesus, not the life and actions of Ignatius of Loyola. My reorientation from religious authority to the primacy of the Spirit is not my innovation but rather Ignatius of Loyola's original inspiration that has deep roots in his *Autobiography* and some aspects of *The Spiritual Exercises*.

The path I outline for experiencing "feast" in both daily prayer and spiritual practice and in religious retreat, begins with a life review and a spiritual autobiography, focused on the ways God's grace has been poured out upon us throughout our lives. It is my hope that *The Feast* offers another way to practice Ignatian spirituality that better resonates with modern life and the direction of the Holy Spirit.

As I have made choices about which aspects of Ignatian spirituality to let go and which to retain, I invite readers to do the same with Ignatius and also *The Feast*.

Joseph F. Duggan

ACKNOWLEDGEMENTS

The Feast as a spiritual practice, as a style of retreat and as this book has been coming to its birth for over three decades, since I left the Society of Jesus. As a book that is significantly about spiritual autobiography, *The Feast* is a journey too. Because this journey has been lived out over several decades, there are many people who have contributed to *The Feast*. It would be fully possible to fill the pages of this book with gratitude for the people by name that I have met through professional life, church, scholarship, activism, and so many other parts of my life — all who contributed to my life, being and presence with God. An exhaustive and comprehensive list is impossible because feast is infused in every minute of daily life and experience beyond my reach but within the celebratory eye of God.

In a more contained way, therefore, I use this space to acknowledge those people and places that have breathed life into me as *The Feast* came into words and experiences. Staying with the metaphor of journey, there is not one journey but many journeys that we take during the course of our lives. I offer gratitude for the Ignatian journey that began with my entrance in the Society of Jesus in 1982 and in a formal way concluded in 1986 when I left the Jesuits; but I stayed on the journey through Jesuit spiritual directors, therapists, and friends. In this way I am especially grateful to my former therapist, Fr. Walter Smith, SJ, who gifted me restoration of life and a gift that constantly renews when he said, "Joe, worship where you are glad," and to Tom Powers, a former Jesuit who once served as my spiritual director and encouraged me to live a life of gratitude. Walter's and Tom's words prophetically anticipated feast through their encouragement of gladness and gratitude in and through my life.

I am grateful to women and men for whom I have had the privilege to be their spiritual guide in the form of a feast long retreat. In 2013 The Rev. Rosa Vera Lindahl placed profound trust in me with her invitation to direct her thirty-day retreat before even a word of this book was written. Never before did I lead the long retreat or a feast retreat. During Rosa's retreat, I began to write this book and then continued to write during the 2014 retreat with Marilyn Collins and Deborah Kempson-Thompson. Each of these women substantively contributed to the feast project as they passionately and transparently share their accounts of their own feasts in this book. Marilyn Collins also designed the beautiful cover of the book, entitled, "Free The Form," that complements my re-forming influences on Ignatian spirituality so that all people may experience the spiritual freedom that Ignatius did as he set out on his pilgrimage.

And the form has been liberated many times over as, for example, with the women of Saint Francis Episcopal Church in Fair Oaks, California, who through their energetic participation in a six-month workshop on Ignatian spirituality and autobiography helped me communicate retreat material for a small group setting in a congregation. There were also many more retreatants who have granted me the privilege to sit at the feast God prepared for them.

Finally *The Feast* journey, like every book that is written and published, has elements of the actual crafting of the book:

I am very grateful for the welcome I received from both Episcopal and Roman Catholic religious communities as reflected by the hospitality of the Anglican brothers at Mount Calvary in Santa Barbara, California, Camp Noel Porter in Tahoe City, California, and by my friend, Fr. Phil Kelly, pastor at St. Frances De Sales Roman Catholic Church in New York City, New York. In these three places, a significant portion of this book was written over a period of two-plus years. Because the book has been written in both Episcopal and Roman Catholic holy spaces, I hope it will inspire Anglicans, Episcopalians, other protestants, and Roman Catholics to find the feast in their diverse lives of faith.

Double blind peer review is the standard for books written by scholars. *The Feast* is not an academic book, but at the same time, I wanted a community of reviewer-readers who either are familiar with me or with *The Feast* and could offer insightful and critical feedback. Stefani Schatz, Rosa Lindahl, Susanna Seltzer, and David Smith all read *The Feast* manuscript in its various versions on the journey towards publication. The affirming and critical feedback I received from my readers was a vital part of the final stages of my writing. With every reader I experienced some unexpected, difficult feedback that often took me a month or more to process. The four readers helped me better understand the deepest recesses of my re-forming spiritual exercise. Their challenges helped *The Feast* in its re-forming resonances.

In the final stages of *The Feast*, The Rev. Christie McManus introduced me to the role of an editor for an author. I will never write another book without sitting down at the outset of the project with an editor. Through Chris' spiritual wisdom and editorial insights I would often receive an email with words such as, "Are you holding back here, Joe?" and "Would you like to say more in this section?"

I am also grateful for Ciara Chivers who copy edited an early draft of *The Feast*.

I am grateful to Melody Stanford who put the final touches on *The Feast* through her commitment to high quality book production processes and also helped me find a way to publish this book.

Although it is uncommon for an author of a book to acknowledge their back cover endorsers -- I want to do so. I chose women and men who I admire and who have spiritually informed my re-forming theology and spiritual practice to be the final readers of my manuscript and to offer their words of encouragement to future readers. I also chose these spiritual leaders and theologians because I was convinced that as they prepared words of endorsement that they would also hold me compassionately accountable – and they did when necessary! For example, during his review, Fr. Roger Haight, SJ, a renowned Jesuit theologian tutored me in greater appreciation of the historical significance of Ignatius of Loyola as a learner in *The Autobiography* and increasing spiritual maturity further along in his faith journey in *The Spiritual Exercises*. Haight's counsel strengthened the quality of my argument. I met Fr. Michael Lapsley, a South African Anglican priest and social justice activist when he preached at All Saints Church, Pasadena, California in 2001. His ministry of healing of memories through his apartheid trauma invites self-disclosure as a spiritual practice. Mary Hunt has been a friend and mentor for several years helping me grow into an activist vocation. Mary's passionate leadership as a feminist theologian was an encounter and reading lens I wanted before this book was published. I knew Dr. Grace Ji-Sun Kim's passionate engagement with the world through the Spirit in protest against all forms of oppression would be a necessary test of my desired integrity of the story I tell. Each of these endorsers has been re-forming theology and spirituality while facing far greater institutional and systemic challenges than I have experienced as a privileged male. I am humbled by their friendship and support for this book.

Finally, I am grateful to *The Feast* readers who choose to take their own spiritual autobiographical journey. May your journey with and through God lead you to places of great joy!

INTRODUCTION TO THE FEAST

Coloring Outside the Lines of Our Spiritual Traditions

I will put my law within them, and I will write it on their hearts; and I will be their God, and they shall be my people. No longer shall they teach one another, or say to each other, "Know the Lord," for they shall all know me, from the least of them to the greatest. —Jer. 31:33b-34a.[1]

These words from Jeremiah support my entire approach to re-forming spirituality, specifically Ignatian spirituality, and the work I have done as a spiritual guide with others. No longer do we need to rely solely on the spiritual wisdom of our Christian foremothers and forefathers. All of us, from the least to the greatest, have the privilege of being in relationship with Jesus and in communion with God through the Holy Spirit.

I first experienced the power of these words when I was only four years old. My mother found me late one winter afternoon in our family's Bronx living room, sitting alone on the sofa, in the dark. The television was off. I was not playing with any of my toys. My mother came into the room, and in a startled tone said, "Joseph, what are you doing sitting all alone in the dark?" Without a moment of hesitation I responded, "Oh, nothing, Mom. I'm just sitting here talking with God."

Later, as an adult, I came to cherish the Reformation's contribution of translating the scriptures into the language of the people, and making them more readily available, so people could read, pray, reflect, and be inspired by the Bible, without mediation through the hierarchy of the church.

---

1. All Bible verses are quoted from the New Revised Standard Version, unless noted otherwise.

The memory of that childhood experience has become one of my signature spiritual stories that helps me remember the pattern of my relationship with God, the pattern of my prayer, and the way I discern God's desires for me. I have found, as I reflect on my life and the stories of various encounters with God, the same pattern repeating itself over and over. Through struggles, questions and doubts, my spiritual practice is to always return to just talking with God and listening to the Spirit. It sounds simple and straightforward, but it is not. Rather, I have learned that talking with God and listening to the Spirit is a dangerous spiritual practice that has interrupted, disrupted and troubled the otherwise calm waters of my life.

In my spiritual journey, I have had to wrestle with the tensions between Ignatius of Loyola's two dominant themes in *The Spiritual Exercises of St. Ignatius* (*Spiritual Exercises*)as expressed in the thirty-day retreat: obedience and spiritual freedom through the direction of the Holy Spirit. These two very different ways of encountering Ignatian spirituality have often been conflated by the Society of Jesus into complete submission to hierarchical authority and obedience. In my decision to leave the Society of Jesus, I acted with spiritual freedom following the Holy Spirit but in disobedience to my religious superiors.

Upon leaving the Society of Jesus, I began an inner exploration of *The Spiritual Exercises* that, over many years, led to my adapting the Ignatian spirituality I received into the re-forming Ignatian spirituality I now live. *Semper reformanda* or "always reforming" echoes the spirit of the protestant reformation. The spirit of constant reform was intended to avoid submission to "popish doctrine," as the reformers described innovations of the Roman Catholic Church not found in scripture or a particular protestant confession. In titling this book and in the spiritual exercise of The Feast, I use the term "re-forming" to underscore the constant and fluid nature of the need to reform. If it were possible and linguistically practical, I would write in other ways that even more boldly express the constant nature of re-forming, such as *re*-re-forming!

Through this re-forming process, I decoupled my spiritual exercises from Ignatius' spiritual exercises to yield those practices in which I routinely find feast.

I didn't attempt to rigidly imitate the spiritual fathers and mothers, but rather to receive their wisdom as an entryway to my own life with God and participation in mission. In this entryway is the feast where our lives constantly intersect Jesus' life and, led by the Spirit, we live in communion with God.

In telling my spiritual autobiography, I had to work to avoid romanticizing the past or glossing over struggles. My guiding principle was to freely enter the struggles of yesterday with the spiritual wisdom of today, while remaining open to deeper healing. I tell my spiritual autobiography, with its re-forming patterns, in the hope that readers will also tell their spiritual autobiographical stories and savor the ways God has repeatedly blessed them and led them to participate in God's mission.

As I started to write my spiritual autobiography, I was drawn to re-read *A Pilgrim's Journey: The Autobiography of Ignatius of Loyola* (*The Autobiography*) to explore its relationship to *The Spiritual Exercises*. In *The Autobiography* Ignatius is a learner and aspirant to the spiritual life whereas in *The Spiritual Exercises* and later in *The Constitutions of the Society of Jesus* he is beginning to develop into a leader of a newly established religious movement. During the period of *The Autobiography* Ignatius' primary guide is the Spirit of God. We find continuity of this emphasis in *The Spiritual Exercises* when Ignatius encourages spiritual directors to get out of the way of the Holy Spirit acting in and through the prayer of the one making the exercises.

My re-reading of *The Autobiography* made my writing project far more complex than I anticipated, because I discovered there an Ignatius I did not expect to meet. The Ignatius I experienced was a passionate lover of the Spirit, committed to know God, undeterred by naysayers, and to serve God in ways that matched his imagination and vision. The Ignatius of *The Autobiography* resonated with my life's journey far better than the Ignatius who I learned about through the practice of authority of my Jesuit religious superiors.

During the time in his life told in *The Autobiography*, Ignatius did not have to submit to a hierarchical authority, as he later required his followers to do. In fact, the man I encountered in *The Autobiography* ignored the advice of many in his pilgrimage. He had no superior except God, and this, perhaps, made him more joyful than the person who was enamored with strict obedience as the basis for mission in and through the Society of Jesus.

That joy was also more consonant with my spiritual experience. In trying to re-form Ignatian spirituality for myself, the word "feast" came to replace Ignatius' words of penance and obedience. Feast describes a way of living in relationship with God. Ignatius' desire was intimacy with God that leads to mission. Feast begins and ends where Ignatius begins and ends; that is, both begin with a desire for intimacy with God, and both end in mission. The difference between the two is in the way we travel from beginning to end, how and by whom we are sent, and how we go on the journey.

Ignatius, in *The Autobiography*, is compelled by the Spirit to go and follow the Spirit. Ignatius and his later companions who made *The Spiritual Exercises* surrender their wills and submit to being sent by the church through religious superiors into mission, a very different way of traveling. In my re-forming, I attempt to recover Ignatius' earliest reliance on the Holy Spirit coupled with discernment, not mediated through sole obedience without question to religious superiors.

The Feast: Re-Forming Ignatian Spirituality offers the breadth of *The Autobiography* and *The Spiritual Exercises* and opens even wider the limitless ways that God's call manifests itself toward service and mission through the radical diversity of individual, human, spiritual encounters with God through the Spirit.

The book cover design, "Free The Form" by Marilyn Collins, captures the way the Spirit of God frees all of our body, mind, and spirit forms to be available for bold, courageous, and loving mission. There are manifold ways of following Ignatius. Jesuits follow Ignatius, the founder of the Society of Jesus. Few, however, are called to be Jesuits. Many more of us are likely to follow Ignatius, the undeterred passionate lover of God who follows the Spirit in the particular ways of God's call.

I hope my book introduces you to the many ways of being inspired by Ignatius of Loyola. Where I have encountered struggles, others have encountered joys. Where I have encountered joys, some have encountered struggles. Each of us must do our own reflection and be faithful to the ways we have spoken to and listened to God throughout our lives. I hope this book empowers you to celebrate your life in God and to share your spiritual autobiography in ways that further encourage your life in God in prayer and mission.

The Feast: Re-forming Ignatian Spirituality is composed of five parts.

In Part One, I begin the book with an account written by Marilyn Collins called "Free the Form," which recounts an artist's experience of leaving behind known forms and finding a new form — re-forming — her art and her spiritual practice on a Feast retreat.

In Part Two, I show the way *The Autobiography* offers a framework for writing and telling our spiritual autobiography and recognizing the spiritual exercises that are most fruitful for each of our individual lives.

In Part Three, I show how Ignatius' autobiographical practices were a starting point for me to write and tell my spiritual autobiography, and then how the autobiography points to my spiritual exercises by illustrating a life-defining pattern of re-forming.

In Part Four, I show the ways I have been re-forming Ignatian spirituality to align with my experience of God with its emphasis on feast.

In Part Five, I invited two other spiritual companions who participated in The Feast retreats to reflect on their autobiographical stories, spiritual exercises, and feast. Each autobiography is different and together they reflect the multiplicity and diversity of discernment questions, autobiographies, spiritual exercises and styles of writing. You will hear experiences of an artist, a poet, and an author.

In the Appendix, I summarize The Feast Resources as a means for readers to enter their own life review, reflect on their spiritual exercises, and follow the Spirit into mission.

The feast is my metaphor for the place where our life stories intersect God's story and God's glory shines through us. In this way, the feast begins for all of us in utero. Through Feast retreats, I invite people to savor the presence of God in their life and be guided by the Spirit, always re-forming the spiritual wisdom they have received from others to best suit their lives and the context in which they live. Feast retreats can be offered in a variety of places, as appetizers or as a full meal, to create a community that shares spiritual seasonings, or a cohort to cook alongside other Feast chefs!

PART I

Free The Form

FREE THE FORM

I was invited to take part in a thirty-day silent retreat. Thirty days seemed like a long time and I was hesitant to commit. I prayed as to whether or not to go. There were responsibilities to tend to, but as time passed, things fell into place. So I decided to go. Since I am an artist, I took along some canvases and acrylic paint. I hadn't used acrylic paint for quite a while, but its advantage is it dries quickly.

My first day was a time of adjustment. My space was adequate, and it included a spot in which to paint. The second day I set up my equipment: easel, paints, 20" x 24" canvases, etc. On the third day, after Morning Prayer, I decided to begin painting.

My first painting was a struggle. I started with my usual approach of drawing organic lines and responding to the forms they create. (I do not paint realistic subjects.) My first attempt wasn't working, so I painted over it and started again. This process took several days. My second attempt was acceptable to me. It reflected my usual style of painting — containing rich colors, unusual organic forms enclosed with black lines, chaotic, with every inch of the canvas covered.

In the meantime, I was encouraged by my spiritual guide to focus on a specific time in the life of Jesus and to understand how my life could be

---

1. Marilyn Collins is an award-winning artist. She has been painting for over twenty years and teaching for fifteen years. She earned her Master of Fine Arts in painting and sculpture from Pennsylvania State University, State College, Pennsylvania, in 1993. She served as Assistant Professor of Art, Kent State University, East Liverpool campus, East Liverpool, Ohio. Her work has been shown at national, state and local levels. She is also a spiritual director.

interwoven into Christ's life. I was particularly drawn to the story of Jesus coming to a village where a woman had been hemorrhaging for years. She touched the garment of Christ and was healed as a result of her faith. Jesus knew that healing power had left him and he asked who had touched him. When she admitted it was she, he welcomed her and called her daughter. I could understand the situation of this woman to a degree. She was rejected because she was considered unclean. I am assuming she was lonely and yearned to be a part of the social life of her community.

When I was growing up I felt a tremendous void. I was cared for, but emotionally I experienced very little love and acceptance. So for many years I searched everywhere for that love and acceptance from many people. The results were disastrous and painful. My heart was battered, wounded, and closed. But I kept running, searching everywhere under all the proverbial rocks. This search has continued my entire life.

During my retreat, I became aware of the image of a figure standing along the road with arms extended. I realize now the figure was Jesus offering his love. But I just ran by thinking, "This is Jesus. I know of you from childhood growing up as a Christian." But I didn't stop running. My addiction would not let me; I needed so much to be accepted and loved.

One day, I was still working on the first painting when these words came to me: "Search for the form and set it free."[2] I was baffled and confused. What did this mean? How can I set the form free? A form is a form and the form is what my paintings are about. I went to my spiritual guide and told him what had happened. He said, "Maybe you are the form." I kept these words in my heart. I finished the first painting in my usual style.

The next day I started the second painting and decided to approach it differently. No drawing of lines to begin (no form), just the applying of paint. This was frightening to me. I certainly did not know what to expect. I chose yellow to begin and it became the background. Three fragile looking red images emerged as I continued. I felt they represented the love of Jesus pouring into my heart. It was a peaceful and joyful painting. It was so totally different from what I usually create. It had only two colors. There was movement but it was free and open. There were no black lines outlining the forms. It wasn't chaotic; instead it was peaceful and without any shapes of general structure.

My third painting also lacked form. The application of paint was free and random. It was purple, blue, joyful, very flowing and free. I was amazed

---

2. The words that came to me are very similar to a quote by Michelangelo, "Every block of stone has a statue inside it and it is the task of the sculptor to discover it," although I did not recognize it at the time.

at what was happening! I couldn't believe I could paint this way. I enjoyed looking at these paintings. They were light in color, free, without form, and seemed ephemeral.

In the meantime, reading about the life of Christ in the scriptures I thought more about the figure of Christ standing along the road with his arms extended. Was that love Jesus was offering? Could it be the love that I have been looking for all my life? The most perfect love and acceptance? Am I to search for the form and set if free? Am "I" the form? Am I supposed to quit running, searching, and just stop? Am I to accept the most perfect love of Jesus as it is being offered to me?

My fourth painting was light red with deeper shades of red, again with no form, free flowing and ephemeral in appearance. I found it to be just as intriguing as the others.

My fifth painting was a lovely blue and green. The difference with this one was that a soft form was beginning to appear, somewhat in the center of the canvas. The rest of the painting was like the previous ones. The form just evolved.

I came to consider what I had done all my life and decided I must stop running and searching. I asked Jesus to heal my heart. To open it up again, to be like it was in the beginning, trusting and innocent, and to heal the wounds of rejection but to be gentle with me. I know it will take time but I am open and waiting.

My sixth painting (cover artwork of this book) is to me the most extraordinary. I started the same way, this time applying brown and tan paint, loosely and responding to it. In the upper portion of the canvas a figure started to evolve. I kept on painting, trying to ignore it. I thought about just painting over it, because when a recognizable image appears, it has to be considered. However, I just kept painting around it. Then I saw a second figure emerge. I studied these figures. Did I paint an image of myself on this canvas? One figure could represent Christ and the other figure could represent me. Christ is behind, with his arms wrapped around me, while I seem to be sitting and resting. I was taken aback by the images. This painting was incredible. I looked tired from running and was being comforted by Christ. The last painting I was able to complete was yellow and brown. I thought about all the rocks metaphorically that I have been looking under. Maybe these images represent them?

I was reading the scripture story about Christ after his resurrection walking on the road to Emmaus. I have asked to stop running and to walk with

Christ on that road and hold on to him. I have asked him to hold me just in case I get the urge to run. Besides, when someone is walking with another, they usually have a conversation. I am praying for that, because I hope to know Jesus, not just know "of" him. I realize now that Jesus and his love are within. I don't have to search for it.

Because of my thirty-day retreat, I realized what I have been doing all my life and also what it has done to others. I know now that Jesus always offers his love. It is within us and it is perfect love. After Jesus left the two men he had walked with on the road to Emmaus, they realized there was fire burning within them when he was with them. The fire within me has been lit. I hope to keep it burning on my continuing journey with Jesus.

The second painting
View full color version at www.thefeastpress.com

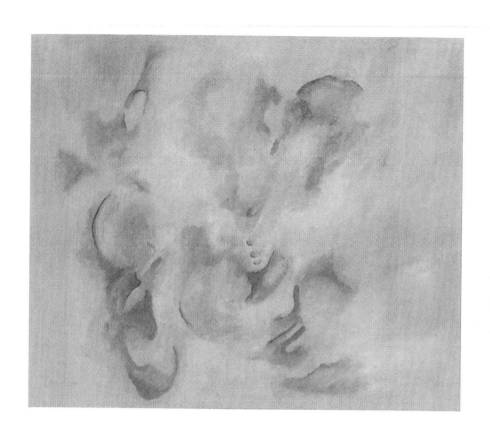

The third painting
View full color version at www.thefeastpress.com

The fourth painting
View full color version at www.thefeastpress.com

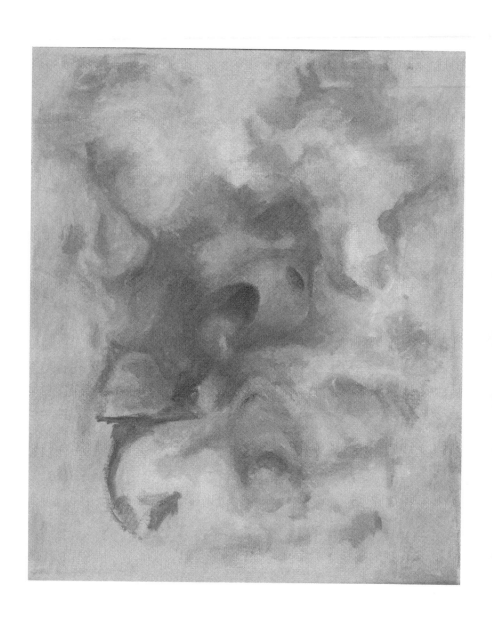

The fifth painting

View full color version at www.thefeastpress.com

PART II

The Autobiography of Ignatius as a Spiritual Autobiographical Exercise

Search me, God and know my heart … — Ps. 139:23a

ONE

Ignatius of Loyola: Moved to Tell the Account of His Interior Life

Ignatius' *Autobiography* offers another lens through which to understand Ignatian spirituality, a different picture than I fully experienced in *The Spiritual Exercises* or through my Jesuit superiors in the Society of Jesus. Through engagement with both manuscripts, however, I see a connection between the life of Ignatius of Loyola, his sense of call, his methods of discernment, and his spiritual exercises. There are many wonderful resources available on *The Autobiography*, some listed in the Bibliography, but a detailed treatment is beyond the scope of this book. Instead, my focus will be the way *The Autobiography* offered me a framework to give an account of my interior life, relationship with Jesus, spiritual exercises, and participation in God's mission.

Attentive to the daily workings of the Holy Spirit in his life, Ignatius recognized at a certain point that it was time to give an account of his story. Ignatius decided to dictate the key elements of his interior life to a fellow companion of Jesus, a Jesuit, an unnamed recorder who throughout this text will be referred to as "the writer." Ignatius selected the writer of his story only after hearing the writer's own "account of soul." The writer sought out Ignatius for spiritual counsel with a concern over his vainglory. In the "Preface of the Writer," he says Ignatius responded, "Refer everything that you do to God; strive to offer Him all the good you find in yourself, acknowledging that this comes from God, and thank Him for it." This response brought the writer to tears.

Ignatius, apparently trusting the integrity of the writer, then shared his struggles with vainglory. Through this initial conversation, Ignatius decided to share more of his interior life with the writer. Ignatius said many had asked him "to give a narrative of his life." The writer said, "Ignatius had resolved to manifest the main points of his interior life up to the present, and had concluded that I was the one to whom he would make these things known." Due to the many demands on his schedule, it took Ignatius from 1553 to 1555 to complete his account.

The Editor, in his short Preface to the 2012 edition of *The Autobiography*, notes, and I fully agree, that *The Autobiography* assists readers with an understanding of Ignatius' interior life for full appreciation of *The Spiritual Exercises*. Indeed, an entire book could be written that traces the parallels between the interior movements of Ignatius' autobiography and *The Spiritual Exercises*.

TWO

The Autobiography: One Way to Give an Account of Our Interior Life

The Autobiography offers one way to make deep, integral connections between our interior lives and the distinctive spiritual exercises that shape our vocation and participation in the mission of God. I invite readers to celebrate their spiritual exercises and to re-form the spiritual wisdom of those who preceded us — including spiritual masters such as Ignatius — with critical resistance to slavishly imitating their particular spiritual exercises and graces.

In my reading of *The Autobiography*, I noted several characteristics that define the connection between Ignatius' spiritual autobiography, his interior life, and his spiritual exercises. I have found these characteristics helpful in writing my spiritual autobiography as well as in the work I do as a spiritual guide with both individuals and congregations.

Relationship — Ignatius gave his account to "the writer."

Life review with the focus of a life-defining discernment question and principles — Ignatius wondered if he should imitate the life of the saints or continue to rise in nobility.

Discernment of spirits — Ignatius listened to his different feelings to determine the movement of the spirits.

Pilgrimage and spiritual differentiation — Ignatius left his "native land and left home."

Incarnation — Ignatius re-forms his received spiritual wisdom and adapts for his needs.

Service — Ignatius has a passion to bring about the kingdom of God through mission.

These characteristics are found in both *The Autobiography* and *The Spiritual Exercises*. In the pages that follow, I offer a few examples from *The Autobiography* and make some suggestions to adapt the spiritual autobiographical account of Ignatius for the writing and telling of our own spiritual autobiographies.

RELATIONSHIP

Ignatius entrusted the account of his interior life to another person, "the writer."

However, both the Editor and the writer point to the hierarchical relationship between Ignatius and the un-named Jesuit companion recording his *Autobiography*. In the "Preface of the Writer," the writer shares an account of a meeting set with Ignatius to continue work on *The Autobiography*. The writer recalls that Ignatius told the writer to meet him in a specific place to continue their conversation, but the writer thought Ignatius would be late, so he sat in a nearby patio. "When St. Ignatius came he reprimanded me because, contrary to obedience, I had not waited for him in the appointed place."

Although Ignatius' relationship with the writer was very hierarchical, the manifestation of each Jesuit's interior life to another became a central characteristic of life in the order. Each year every Jesuit around the world is required to give a manifestation of conscience to his local superior. While the writer's role for Ignatius was only to record, later this characteristic evolved in the Society of Jesus beyond passive listener into a real, lived relationship.

In this book, the relational nature of telling the account of my interior life continues to evolve and expand. The relational nature of giving my account has been central to the way my spiritual autobiography has opened up and blossomed over many years of practice. Throughout my spiritual life, it has been important for me to have either a spiritual companion or a community to share my faith and story. In writing this book, I give my account in a different way, to a broader audience.

I am always learning to tell my spiritual autobiography as I listen to other people share their spiritual autobiographies. In a variety of contexts, I have learned different ways of telling and listening, but few have matched the intimacy of sharing this evolving book with spiritual companions and

Stefani, my lifetime soul mate. When I have shared my spiritual autobiography with those who know and love me, I also receive the critical feedback I need to go deeper with my story. Acceptance and love do not lead to a lack of accountability, but rather what my friend Rosa Lindahl calls "compassionate accountability." Compassionate accountability invites two people into a place of generous reciprocity of spiritual reflection where each guides and is guided by the other. In knowing one another and our stories well, we are able to compassionately hold each other accountable.

LIFE REVIEW WITH THE FOCUS OF A LIFE-DEFINING DISCERNMENT QUESTION

The Autobiography offers a compact, sixty-one page account of Ignatius of Loyola's life. His account begins with an injury at Pamplona that almost caused his death. Due to the care of excellent doctors, his devotion to St. Peter, and his determination to live, he recovered.

During his recovery, Ignatius asked for some books to pass the time. He specifically asked for romances, but no such books were available where he was staying. "They gave him instead, *The Life of Christ*, by Rudolf, the Carthusian, and another book, called *The Flowers of The Saints*, both in Spanish."[1] Through these readings, Ignatius began to turn his mind and heart toward spiritual things.

Ignatius spent his days fantasizing about romance and nobility. In addition to these thoughts, "While perusing the life of Our Lord and the saints, he began to reflect, saying to himself: What if I should do what St. Francis did? What if I should act like St. Dominic?"[2]

He thus informally submitted to a "life review" as he looked back over his life, just as in the first week of *The Spiritual Exercises*, he invites retreatants to do a life review in preparation for a general confession. Here I use Ignatius' term "life review" as a way to recall patterns of discernment and grace in preparation to write a spiritual autobiography. What I call a "life-defining discernment question" gave shape to the rest of Ignatius' life and vocation.

Through Ignatius' life-defining discernment question he is attentive to the movement of the Spirits in his life, as I will address more fully in the next section.

---

1. *A Pilgrim's Journey: The Autobiography of St. Ignatius of Loyola* (San Bernardino, CA: Renaissance Classics, 2012), 2.

2. Ibid., 3.

Ignatius' life-defining discernment question was: will I continue in my life as a noble soldier and man who enjoys worldly pleasures, or will I follow Christ? Ignatius' experience led to his rules for discernment of spirits. Ignatius' question and discernment, in turn, led me to claim my own spiritual exercises and not simply follow his from the sixteenth century.

The life-defining discernment question for Ignatius followed his health crisis. My life-defining discernment question unfolded much more slowly. Through thirty years of spiritual direction, thirteen years of marriage, ten years of ordained ministry and seven years of individual therapy I have experienced over and over my pattern of received grace as well as my resistances to grace. To name my life-defining discernment question, I have had to look at my patterns of grace, when I moved forward easily, when I resisted, and when I just struggled in place without resolution. Ultimately, I understood my life-defining discernment question to be: when do I need to question authority; when do I need to re-form what I've received from others to restore my life in communion with God?

I know answering this question involves listening to the Spirit, over-reliance on my own planning, and yearning to participate in discerning relationships and communities. The times when my question arises are often a break from my routine expectations and/or institutional norms and lead to a process of re-forming.

Ignatius' life-defining discernment question is the connecting tissue that helped him encounter God and tell his spiritual autobiographical story, describe his spiritual exercises, communicate his theology, and demonstrate his response to God's invitation to participate in God's mission. In a similar manner my life-defining discernment question has helped me to write my spiritual autobiography, claim my spiritual exercises, communicate my theology, and demonstrate my response to God's invitation to participate in God's mission.

DISCERNMENT OF SPIRITS

Ignatius of Loyola got great satisfaction from reflecting on the lives of the saints and imagining how he would imitate them.

These heroic resolutions remained for a time, then other vain and worldly thoughts followed. This succession of thoughts occupied him for a long while, those about God alternating with those about the world. But in these thoughts there was a difference. When he thought of world things it gave him great pleasure, but afterward he found himself dry and sad. But when he thought of journeying to Jerusalem, and of living only on herbs, and practising austerities, he found pleasure not only while thinking of them, but also when he had ceased.[3]

Ignatius did not immediately recognize a significant difference in the variety of his feelings. Then, through the inspiration of the Holy Spirit, Ignatius began to prayerfully reflect on how his feelings differed with different thoughts.

He learned by experience that one train of thought left him sad, the other joyful. This was the first reasoning on spiritual matters. Afterward when he began *The Spiritual Exercises*, he was enlightened and understood … about the discernment of spirits. When gradually he recognized the different spirits by which he was moved, one, the Spirit of God, the other, the devil, and when he had gained no little spiritual light from the reading of pious books, he began to think more seriously of his past life, and how much penance he should do to expiate his past sins.[4]

Ignatius is attentive to the movement of the Spirit, as he discerned where God was leading him at the outset of his *Autobiography* as well as throughout his life. He tests his life-defining discernment question by listening to the Spirit and being attentive to his feelings.

Learning to trust the Spirit has taught me that I need to trust that God is present, even when I experience the discomfort of disruptions and spiritual turbulence in my life. In my experience, the best pilots are those who address the turbulence passengers experience. I know that in the absence of a sensitive pilot who mentions the turbulence, I tend to think the plane is going to fall out of the sky and we are all going to die! Of course I know, rationally, that planes don't fall out of the sky due to turbulence. Sensitive, competent pilots normalize my experience of turbulence. With many years of travel, most of the time I am now able to be in the midst of turbulence and differentiate between my feelings of imminent crisis and my knowledge of the reality.

Similarly, sensitive and competent spiritual guides and other religious leaders have narrated and led me through Spirit-led disruptions and spiritual turbulence. When I have been solely in search of the sweetness of God's presence, I have sometimes missed the call of the Spirit to some uncomfortable places. If sweetness had not been my sole test of God's presence, I would

---

3. Ibid., 3.

4. Ibid., 3-4.

have discovered the presence of God in some places I might not have been initially drawn to go. For too much of my life, I associated spiritual turbulence with the absence of God, and resisted following the Spirit into those creative spaces where I would have had abundant opportunities to stretch my knowledge, love, and service of God. As I have matured spiritually, I have been able to self-narrate through the turbulence of my felt chaos and dare to seek beyond my tame baseline faith. Most often these times of spiritual turbulence have led to re-forming and feast.

Ignatius' reliance on the sweetness of grace and the prolonged good feelings associated with following Christ led to his rules for discernment of spirits. One of his time-honored discernment principles is not to make a decision in either consolation or desolation but only in times of tranquility. Ignatius' discernment principle helps me avoid anxious decisions, but tranquility alone has also led me to avoid the disruptive risks often associated with Spirit-led calls.

PILGRIMAGE, LEAVING HOME AND SPIRITUAL DIFFERENTIATION

Chapter II of *The Autobiography* is entitled "Ignatius Leaves His Native Land — What He Did at Montserrat And At Manresa." Ignatius opens this chapter with an account of the beginning of his pilgrimage to Jerusalem:

Ignatius, starting from his father's house, set upon his journey on horseback. ... His brother desired to accompany him as far as Ogna ... Having prayed some time at the shrine for new strength for his journey, leaving his brother at Ogna at the house of his sister, to whom he paid a short visit, he journeyed on to Navarre.[5]

Several lines later Ignatius reported, "Then dismissing his two remaining servants, he rode forth alone from Navarre in the direction of Montserrat, a mountain town of Catalonia in the Northern part of Spain."[6] For Ignatius, leaving home is an expression of his spiritual maturity and spiritual differentiation. The brevity of description from Ignatius about his act of leaving home has similar parallels to the hidden life of Jesus recorded in less than a line of Holy Scripture. Nevertheless, Ignatius set out alone on his pilgrimage, and his setting out, in part, marked his spiritual differentiation from his family.

Spiritual differentiation is a prerequisite for a mature spirituality. The process of becoming an adult is a process of differentiation from one's parents.

---

5. Ibid., 5.

6. Ibid.

When I was a child, I yearned for the affirmation of my parents. I recognized early on that the more I complied with their wishes, the greater my feelings of affirmation. The differentiation process began when my desires began to shift, and the ways I sought to be affirmed changed. Differentiated adults develop their own unique identity and way of being in the world. Many parents have empathy for the differentiation process of their children, since they, too, differentiated from their parents. Parents sometimes initially grieve their loss of both intimacy and control, as their adult children differentiate and set out to craft their own lives, but healthy parents and children come to accept and celebrate the maturing of the child into adult.

More challenging for me has been the process of spiritual differentiation. When I was spiritually young, I sought the affirmation of my spiritual masters. Becoming a spiritual adult has been a slow process of differentiation from those spiritual masters. Not unlike my differentiation from my parents, the process has not been without struggle and cost to claim my distinctive, grace-filled identity.

Leaving the Society of Jesus was a significant occasion for me to differentiate spiritually. However, when authority dominates the church-member relationship, there cannot be spiritual differentiation. If my Jesuit religious superiors could have been present to the changes I was undergoing, could have grieved with me and celebrated the changes in my commitments as a Jesuit, that differentiation might have happened in a healthier manner that contributed to the life of the community.

In fact, spiritual differentiation is most likely to take place in the context of healthy relationships in spiritual communities. A differentiated spirituality calls people and communities to hold each other compassionately accountable without sole dependence on authority or power. Differentiated people and communities are not divided into spiritual masters who expect and subjects who conform and comply. When spirituality becomes no longer about subjects' compliance to their masters, all are liberated to be available to the Spirit of God with energy for God's mission. The creativity of God is unleashed.

In the parent-child relationship, both parent and child must change for healthy differentiation to emerge and flourish. If the parent resists differentiation, the child has at least three options. The adult child can continue to be the child and fail to flourish as a differentiated adult. The adult child can break off the relationship with their parent and sever their bond. Or, sometimes, the adult child can claim her or his adult identity without severing the relationship and, if the parent can tolerate the discomfort, they can gradually move over time toward a healthy relationship of two adults.

In my experience, churches often resist Christians taking this same kind of self-responsibility, instead maintaining a church-as-parent relationship with their members. Faithful people can submit to the authority of the church and their superiors without question. Alternatively, adults can sever their relationship with the church. The greatest challenge is to negotiate the relationship in ways that lead to healthy differentiation that grows the membership of the church.

The decline of many congregations and seminaries is a result of the church's resistance to healthy spiritual differentiation. The healthy character of churches at local, national and international levels of communion requires a reciprocal participation in the process of spiritual differentiation. Too often, much of the burden for spiritual differentiation lies with churches' individual members. Some spiritual leaders lack the spiritual freedom to use their authority in ways that lead to healthy members and communities. Spiritually free leaders do not cling to authority, but rather, use it as a gift to care and pastorally companion, leaving generous space for spiritual growth, change and development.

Nonetheless, the process of spiritual differentiation continues for me in The Episcopal Church, as well as with my congregation. In Part III I further discuss my decision to leave the Society of Jesus and the impact of my decision on my spiritual life and re-forming Ignatian spirituality.

INCARNATION

The Autobiography reflects Ignatius' historical time and place. The recommendation of the Editor of *The Autobiography* to imitate Ignatius is impractical, given the significant differences between the sixteenth century context of Ignatius and our twenty-first century context. The incarnational dimension leads to a dynamic re-forming process that is deeply embedded in the Ignatian spiritual tradition, though this aspect is not addressed in *The Autobiography*. In *The Constitutions of The Society of Jesus,* Ignatius describes the way he sought papal approval and dispensation for Jesuits to do the daily office outside of the traditional practice of the monastic choir.[7] The vision of Ignatius was for his companions of Jesus (the Jesuits) to be contemplatives

---

7. *The Constitutions of the Society of Jesus and their Complementary Norms* (Saint Louis: The Institute of Jesuit Sources, 1996), p.256.

in action. He knew his companions would be active, and that their life would be ordered in a different daily pattern than monks in the monasteries of the world. Through his understanding of the spiritual life of the Jesuits and their expected experience, he sought reformation of a time-honored spiritual exercise. Through the centuries, Jesuits recite the divine office privately as they have time in the course of their daily activities.

Similarly, Ignatius anticipated that *The Spiritual Exercises* in their unaltered form would be inaccessible to most people, because they would be unable to take off four or more weeks from their labor to make the retreat. Ignatius offered an accommodation through the Nineteenth Annotation, where *The Spiritual Exercises* are made with a spiritual director in the time available within the daily activities of life and work. Both of these examples have been sources of encouragement for my own attentiveness to my spiritual needs in the context of this time, place, and history as well as spiritual disposition, patterns of grace, and desires.

Each time I reflect on my spiritual autobiography, there is an opening up of new insights through grace. It has taken time to understand and appreciate the way the Spirit has been working in and through the rich complexities of my life. In times of active transition, it has been difficult to process and narrate the life within that is happening. All my stories are complex and defy simple narration. The effort to narrate my spiritual autobiography further deepens my communion with God.

SERVICE

Ignatius was ahead of his time, and as a sixteenth century founder of the Society of Jesus, Ignatius had a missional spirit and energy where all his aspirations pointed to companionship with Jesus and participation in the mission of God. In *The Autobiography*, Ignatius frequently speaks of his "ardent desire of serving God" and "the great things he would do for the love of God."[8] Throughout *The Autobiography*, Ignatius offers an account of the many risks he took on his pilgrimage to prepare himself for mission.

Over difficult terrain, Ignatius travelled by foot, boat, and many other means of transportation to get to his desired destinations. Often along the way, Ignatius met those who urged caution and communicated fear to him. Nonetheless, fear never stopped Ignatius on his journey; he would travel on

---

8. Ibid.

trust in the providence of God. Along the way he begged for alms, fasted, and ate only bread for days. The risks Ignatius took were often so great, that he was more than once falsely accused and brought to trial. He always received a favorable judgment, but these challenges tested his will and proved his fierce determination to serve as a companion of Jesus.

In the Society of Jesus, a significant emphasis is put on Jesuits being assigned to a specific mission by their religious superior whereas Ignatius goes on pilgrimage because he is compelled by the Spirit to do so, not because he is sent by another, i.e. his religious superior.

Ignatius assumes the authority to send his companions, but his authority to send is not based on his imitation of being sent by a religious superior. The Ignatius of *The Autobiography* might never have had the experiences he had on his pilgrimage if he had been a Jesuit under sometimes the arbitrary wills of Jesuit superiors!

PART III

Writing My Spiritual Autobiography

I will go to the altar of God, the God who gives joy to my youth.
— Roman Missal, 1962, Introductory Rites of the Mass

THREE

The Impossible Task of Writing Our Spiritual Autobiography

Like Ignatius of Loyola, I did not set out to tell the story of my interior life to the entire world! Several years ago Ed Soja, Distinguished Professor of Urban Planning at the London School of Economics, stated, during a lecture at the University of Manchester, that the greatest writing challenge is to give an account of one's own life. Soja said it is virtually impossible to write our autobiographical stories in ways that yield the "real-time" deep complexity of multiple layers including the intellectual, the emotional and the spiritual. One of the reasons it has been so difficult to tell a coherent account of my life is because the Spirit has not acted in a straight line moving me from point A to point B in consecutive steps. My plans often have had a consecutive, linear quality, whereas the Spirit has been more comfortable in the chaos.

One way I have addressed the challenge is to tell only a portion of my story. Ignatius does not tell his whole life story in *The Autobiography*. After reading *The Autobiography*, we still do not know many details of Ignatius' life. In his partial account, he tells those stories that help us better understand his role as founder of the Society of Jesus and the author of *The Spiritual Exercises*. In the next few chapters I offer a partial account of my spiritual autobiography to help readers better understand my ministry of re-forming received spiritual wisdom.

Over the years I have been invited to write my spiritual autobiography as part of various discernment processes with which I have participated. I wrote my spiritual autobiography for entrance into the Society of Jesus, for admission into Clinical Pastoral Education, to each seminary and theological school I have attended, and as part of therapy I have undergone with some psychotherapists. The first autobiography I wrote in 1982; the most recent one was in preparation for this book. Each autobiographical version rendered a picture of my spiritual life, as well as that of the autobiography's recipient audience.

The spiritual autobiography I wrote for entrance into the Society of Jesus in 1982 reflected the way I heard my call to become a Jesuit priest. As part of the application process, I was asked to write about how I heard the call to be a Jesuit through my life experiences, including family, school, work, and parish. The autobiography I wrote was a chronological account of the blessings I experienced through my family. I reflected on the way each family member inspired me to aspire to become a Jesuit priest.

My spiritual autobiography told the story of my "good" Roman Catholic family, where vocations to the church have flourished for generations. Every Jesuit on the admissions committee affirmed the quality of my spiritual autobiography and the blessing of my family. I affirmed my family, my family affirmed me, and the Society of Jesus' admission's committee affirmed my spiritual autobiography.

A few years later I was asked to write a spiritual autobiography as part of the Clinical Pastoral Education (CPE) application process. Due to a combination of my laziness and an inflated sense of the quality of my Jesuit spiritual autobiography, I decided to use basically the same manuscript with very few changes, apart from a few additional chronological details. At my interview, Joan Hemenway, the then CPE supervisor at Memorial Sloan Kettering in New York City, described my spiritual autobiography as a "fantasy." Joan asked me, "Where is your pain, suffering and doubt?" I had no idea what she was talking about. The interview did not go well and I was not accepted into the program. Joan's direct question had a deep and lasting impact on me. It took a decade and more to answer Joan's question through time in therapy, spiritual direction, and my own readiness to explore the background story.

While the Jesuits read an autobiographical story about manifold blessings, Joan heard an untold, silent story tucked away in my unconscious, out of my reach. She read an autobiography that lacked any mention of my own spiritual identity. My lack of differentiation from my family signaled to Joan the way my spiritual identity likely had been subordinated and erased by my family. Joan challenged me to go find my story. I was accepted by another CPE program where I began the multi-year work to find parts of my story.

Organizations and counselors give subtle and sometimes not-so-subtle messages about what they hope and expect to read in candidates' spiritual autobiographies. The Society wanted to read about the way a candida. family was a blessing. Joan, as a CPE supervisor, wanted to read a self-critica reflection of a candidate's spiritual identity. Later I studied for ordination in The Episcopal Church at the Episcopal Divinity School, which has strong values against racism. That institution wanted an account of the ways I perpetuated racism in my autobiography. One psychotherapist invited me to tell my spiritual-sexual embodiment story.

The autobiographical expectation seems to be associated with an organization's identity, their autobiographical story, their theology, and a spoken, implied or subtle expectation that those who seek to be a part of their community will fully comply with its dominant values. Each time I wrote for a different organizational recipient, I learned important autobiographical competencies including blessing (Jesuits), critical self-reflection (CPE), power analysis (EDS) and embodiment (psychotherapists).

In every spiritual autobiography I have written, I, in some sense, complied with the expectations of others, and in doing so distanced myself from the power of God's presence within me. I sometimes willingly forced my call into pre-determined acceptable and legitimized calls. It has taken a lifetime to find spiritual freedom through the struggles of living my particular call and vocation. The blessings, self-critical reflection, power analysis, and embodiment lacked one critical autobiographical characteristic: the recipient of my spiritual autobiography was never in relationship with me in that analysis, critical reflection, or embodiment. The Society of Jesus, CPE, seminaries and several (not all) psychotherapists each served in unilateral roles as evaluator and hierarchical overseers who assessed my level of compliance. In these cases, a lack of reciprocity did not engender in me trust, vulnerability, or surrender of my will to the community's desires for me.

FOUR

Leaving Home and Re-Forming

In this section I share a few life stories that point to the ways I have been leaving home and, in the process, re-forming received spiritual wisdom and tradition. These stories show the direct relationship between my spiritual autobiography and my spiritual exercise of re-forming. In the stories I share, a life-defining discernment question found in *The Autobiography* of Ignatius helps me narrate my partial spiritual autobiography. My life-defining question is different from the question Ignatius asked. Nevertheless, several of his other autobiographical characteristics come into play in my spiritual autobiography, especially a re-forming ministry grounded in taking risks to question authority through the Spirit.

NATURAL LAW AND MY BIRTH

My life-defining discernment question was already a part of my life when I was in the womb, and was present in the story I told in the Introduction about just talking to God as a four-year-old. My mom was 48 years old when she was pregnant with me, after having given birth to four other children. Her age contributed to a high-risk pregnancy. A few hours before my mom expected to give birth to me, our family doctor/obstetrician visited with my dad to inform him that he might not be able to save my mom and me. Consistent with Roman Catholic principles of natural law, the doctor explained that he would save me and let my mom die.

The church's laws took precedent over my parents' wishes without mutual conversation. My parents were not a part of the decision surrounding my birth. They were made invisible in the decision-making process. They were expected to be obedient to church law and trust their doctor's recommendation. The expected norm was silence and passive obedience.

THE NAME I WAS GIVEN AND MY REAL NAME: JOSEPH FRANCE(I)S

Our family doctor was able to bring me into the world and also save my mom. It was a traumatic delivery that required my mom to have several transfusions of blood. We remained in the hospital for three weeks. During our time in the hospital, I received an emergency baptism by one of the nurses. The nurse pinned a medal of St. Frances Cabrini to my hospital gown as she said the words of baptism over me. Due to my challenged birth, the nurse chose St. Frances Cabrini because the saint had been born prematurely and remained a weak and sickly child challenged by health issues throughout her life.

St. Frances Cabrini was a celebrated woman of faith who became a saint in 1946, the first citizen of the United States to ever be canonized. Frances was born into a large family in Lodi, Italy. Frances took the name Xavier after Francis Xavier when she was confirmed, in admiration of his missionary zeal. Frances Cabrini is the patron saint of immigrants, due to her leadership in the establishment of orphanages for Italian immigrants in the United States and around the world.

When we were released from the hospital, Fr. Joseph Kozlowski baptized me Joseph Francis. Frances was spelled Francis on all the documents because I was a boy. Later, however, I began celebrating having a feminine name alongside my other, masculine names. I often think about the possibility of changing my name back to Frances to reflect the name given to me. Returning to the name Frances would be symbolic, and would visibly acknowledge my resistance to the way we too often polish the edginess of our lives to conform to gender and other institutional expectations.

My parents' inclination to comply with institutional expectations was present in both my birth and naming. My response to their and my own compliance has, over the years, evolved into my desire to be Frances, after my patron Saint Frances Cabrini.

DARING TO CLIMB THE HIGH ALTAR

I spent a good portion of my childhood going to church with my mother. My mother was always reserved in church and at home. She was always proud of the way her children were so obedient and courteous when we were in stores or church. She loved to tell stories of our obedience, even in a china shop, where most children would be a great risk to the precious contents. We Duggan children were docile and obedient. We also were simply too afraid of our mother not to be docile and obedient, as we would be quickly scolded and punished if we exhibited any other behavior. As the youngest in the family, I was consistently compliant, following a legacy of docility and obedience, especially in church. At the same time, I spent most of my childhood living in my head, asking questions like, "What if I were not docile, obedient, and invisible?" One day, when I was five years old, I could no longer stand life in my head, and I dared, for a few minutes, to live my cerebral life on the outside. We were in another local parish church near where we lived. The church had a life-size child Jesus, royally dressed, that I recall as the Infant of Prague, the boy Jesus. The statue was on one of the side altars. The boy Jesus was dressed in many layers of garments with a royal crown on top of his head.

My mother was busy talking to a neighbor. I made my way to the front of the church, climbed up on the altar and lifted the Infant of Prague's garments to see what was underneath. I remember knowing at some level that I was breaking a boundary, but I did not see the boundary in the same way as my mother. At one point my mother's attention shifted to the altar. My mother, hardly recognizing her otherwise angelic son screamed, "What are you doing, Joseph?" I quickly responded, "I had to see what was underneath."

"Get down from there right away," she said as she rushed down the aisle, "Get down, get down, what has gotten into you?" I dropped the Infant's garment as she continued, "You have never done anything like this before."

I clumsily got down from the altar. As I climbed down, I clearly remember an inner feeling that one day I would be back, and my church would be a place where there would be freedom to metaphorically look underneath and ask re-forming questions!

FIRST HOLY COMMUNION

I was a painfully shy child, notwithstanding my ability to climb altars! I spent my entire first- and second-grade classes never raising my hand once. In the second half of the second-grade year, in February, Sister Helen was preparing us for our First Holy Communion. We learned about all seven sacraments. When Sister Helen talked about each of the sacraments, she explained the way the sacrament was God's way of loving us. When she got to marriage and Holy Orders (ordination to the priesthood), Sister Helen said, "Now God loves some people into marriage and some people into Holy Orders."

I may not have spoken in class, but I was always listening, and that statement did not sit right with me, so I raised my hand! Sister Helen had to turn to her seating chart to look for my name, because I was not a familiar speaker in class. She hesitantly said my name.

"Joseph?"
"Yes, Sister."
"Joseph, are you all right?"
"Yes, Sister."
"Joseph, do you have question?"
"Yes, Sister. What if God really loves you a whole lot and wants you to be married and be a priest?"
"Joseph, God would never love you in that way."

I responded, "I don't understand." Sister Helen, whom I adored as a teacher, said, "Well Joseph, perhaps it will become clearer to you as we continue our lessons." It never became clear!

Looking back on these four stories I see that they give evidence to my life-defining question very early in my life. As I grew older, the autobiographical story of my life in the Society of Jesus, as well as my decision to leave the Society, and the manner and process in which I left, collectively and irrevocably continued to shape that question and my relationship to the church and to God. Again the question is when to question authority in order to re-form for restoration of life in communion with God.

FIVE

Leaving the Society of Jesus

The story of my leaving the Society of Jesus and my relationship with my superiors has had a profound consequence on my life and is the sole reason I was led, over a period of three decades, to re-form *The Spiritual Exercises* and Ignatian spirituality. Thus it is essential to tell this part of my autobiography for this book to be understandable.

LOSS OF WORDS FOR MY MOST INTIMATE SPIRITUAL EXPERIENCES

Earlier I mentioned the difficulty in telling a full autobiographical account in ways that offer an exact verbatim of our experiences as we live them. Even exact verbatims do not offer a complete narrative of the experience as it happened. In earlier drafts of this book, I included a three-month exchange of correspondence between my Jesuit religious superiors and me leading up to my departure from the Society of Jesus. The collected correspondence took thirty plus pages.

I wanted to include the correspondence as a way to avoid editing the experience by either dismissing it as a story of little consequence or by an over-dramatizing it as if it happened yesterday and nothing else that has happened has had equal significance. The most dramatic telling of the story risks losing the maturity of the man I am today to the youthful, and, in some way, naïve and innocent Jesuit I was in the late eighties.

Some early readers identified with the drama, while other readers were overwhelmed by too much detail ,and those readers closest to me struggled to find the man they know me to be today.

Ed Soja was right; it is impossible to tell our most intimate and meaningful stories in ways that both repeat the felt experience in the minds and hearts of those who hear our accounts and yet reveal the maturity achieved through integration of the experience. There may be another book I write at another time about the deep connections, for me, between anger, grief and feast.

When I tell my spiritual autobiographical story, I have difficulty finding words to express my deepest feelings and my sense of what my story means. I am able to easily tell the chronological details. If I owned the letters from the Society of Jesus, I would publish them for full disclosure as an appendix for you to be the judge. Without a full chronology and verbatim, exact correspondence, the story cannot be told in the ways my whole spiritual life has been transformed. Also, words cannot embody my experience with God and the way the Spirit has worked through my spiritual autobiography.

Nonetheless, I tell the story I have access to, not so much out of a desire that you know about me, but rather so we all participate in the struggle to tell each other where God shows up in our lives and how God is the reason for the choices we make. I bear witness to the power of God in my life. I bear witness to the way God was and has been the light and joy and also in the midst of profound struggle, darkness, alienation and rejection.

PROTEST(ANT) TURN

I entered the Society of Jesus in August 1982, and, although I made my religious profession of vows in August 1984, I struggled with Jesuit life and community. I made it through two years of philosophy (1984-86) but not without great emotional and physical cost. In the formation period leading from philosophy to regency (a three-year teaching assignment), I began an appeals process to my superiors to seek a different assignment, one where I thought I would have the opportunity to better integrate my experiences in an affirming Jesuit community. I was looking for a way to hit the "pause button" without the necessity of making a decision to leave. At the time, I wanted to stay in the Society of Jesus. I just wanted time apart from the pain I was feeling. I wanted to be nurtured. I wanted to be heard.

In my letters to my religious superiors, I outlined my personal struggles. I asked for an apostolic assignment that would allow me to assimilate what

I had already experienced of Jesuit formation. Alternatively, I asked for a leave of absence to put my struggles in perspective. I saw these requests as an opportunity for emotional and spiritual healing. My superiors ignored my pleas for assistance.

Denied the desired change, I looked in the pattern of my life and, not seeing any other changes in the immediate future, I defiantly withdrew from my classes. I withdrew without the permission of my superiors with full knowledge that my action would heighten their attention to my needs and that there would also likely be disciplinary consequences. I was reprimanded, and I was reminded of my need to be obedient.

At that time I also made a decision to leave the house of formation with the permission of my local superiors. At this point I was well on my way to leaving the Society of Jesus, but since I was caught in my own reactive state, I lacked the benefit of discernment in community with my superiors.

I even wrote to the Superior General of the Society of Jesus. I shared with the General my struggles and exhaustion. I told him I "could no longer continue to live in unnecessary pain" and I explained why the vowed life in its current circumstances was no longer suitable to my inner spiritual disposition. Having poured out my heart in all my letters, I was profoundly disappointed in my superiors' perfunctory replies. For example, the response I received from the Superior General was in part:

I am deeply concerned for your very obvious suffering. And I sincerely wish I could be of help to you, so that you might move through this pain to a happier time of your life ... You use the word discernment. I have the impression you do not know that a Jesuit receives his missions from the Society and that the term discernment, for a Jesuit, therefore, is not a decision but rather is advice given to the superior, who makes the decision .... .

Nine months after I signed my dispensation papers I read in a then-current issue of *Studies in The Spirituality of Jesuits,* an article by John Staudenmaier, SJ, who said:

"As we help candidates and men in the early stages of Jesuit life to interpret their experience, we do well if we pay more attention to their deepening maturity about and their increased access to their hope and despair than to evidence they can conform their behavior to Jesuit norms ... If we do not allow time for vulnerability and confusion of the inner journey, we run the risk of driving vital and gifted men from our midst or of encouraging premature conformity. Such a short cut can lead to a life of sterile rigidity or postpone the encounter with hope and despair until it erupts later in life. Neither outcome represents the Jesuit charism.[9]

Father Staudenmair's words brought much comfort to me at the time. With his words I knew I was not alone in my struggles.

As I left, my superiors placed sole accountability on me and my lack of spiritual freedom to be an obedient Jesuit. Over time I have come to recognize that my local superiors, and even Father General, also lacked spiritual freedom. I have come to see that the only spiritual freedom I lacked was to be an obedient Jesuit. In the Jesuits, spiritual freedom was equivalent to submission of the individual's will to comply with mandated corporate obedience of religious superiors. I chose to be disobedient to pursue spiritual and emotional wholeness. The Society could not acknowledge that I did not lack spiritual freedom but was seeking restoration of my life. My failing, if anything, was disobedience to the Jesuit definition of spiritual freedom.

YEARS OF REFLECTION AND INTEGRATION

In the years after I left the Society of Jesus, I immersed myself in the writings of the Society. I reread the *Constitutions of the Society of Jesus,* to which I had been introduced during my first year of novitiate formation. Ignatius wrote in "The Rules for Thinking with The Church":

What seems to me white, I will believe black if the hierarchical Church so defines. For I must be convinced that in Christ our Lord, the bridegroom, and in His spouse the Church, only one Spirit holds sway, which governs and rules for the salvation of souls. For it is by the same Spirit and Lord who gave the Ten Commandments that our Holy Mother Church is ruled and governed.[10]

These foundational words of Ignatius have become a shorthand way of describing to others why I left the Society of Jesus. I now tell people that I left because I do not accept that spiritual freedom prepares one to surrender and submit to blind obedience to their religious superiors. For me spiritual freedom leads to constant reform and wholeness of life.

Though I lacked the language at the time, now I realize that leaving the Society of Jesus, and my obedience to the felt Spirit acting in my life, was another important step in leaving home and re-forming my received spiritual

---

9. John M. Staudenmaier, "United States Technology and Adult Commitment," *Studies In The Spirituality of Jesuits,* Vol. 19, No. 1 (January 1987), 31-32.

10. *The Spiritual Exercises of St. Ignatius, trans.* Louis J. Puhl (Chicago: Loyola Press, 1951), 160.

wisdom. In the process of leaving the Society, I was beginning my journey toward leaving the Roman Catholic Church and becoming a Protestant. This final and definitive act of leaving home would not come for another fifteen years, when I was received into The Episcopal Church in 2001. At the same time as I was leaving behind my received spiritual wisdom from family, the Society of Jesus and the Roman Catholic Church, I was also carrying forward with me central characteristics of *The Autobiography*. Like Ignatius, who was compelled to respond to the Spirit moving within his life, I felt compelled by the Spirit in the journey I was on.

Shortly after leaving the Society of Jesus, I shared my journey with Fr. Walter Smith, SJ, who gave me the gift of two years of therapy (1987-89) and restored me to a place of wholeness through his patient listening and compassionate understanding. For a short period of time at General Theological Seminary in 1987, I met Dr. Richard Schaull, who introduced me to liberation theology and the work of Leonardo Boff. Schaull wrote on my final paper, "The Ecclesiology of Base Christian Communities," "You have captured the early vision of Protestantism. I hope you find the community you seek and yearn for in this paper." In meeting with Fr. Smith, I was able to find the spiritual freedom to pursue life outside the Roman Catholic Church. My practice of differentiation and re-forming did not cease with my separation from the Society of Jesus and the Roman Catholic Church. My spiritual maturation process has always been dependent on my commitment to differentiation and re-forming.

NEW LIFE IN MISSION

Throughout my whole life, I have been talking with God and listening to the Spirit.

Leaving the Society of Jesus was definitely due to a sense of the Spirit leading me to the restoration of my life and, at the same time, making me more aware of a need for re-forming Ignatian spirituality. I have a great sense of camaraderie with Ignatius of Loyola. He did not go on the journey to Jerusalem to become the founder of the Society of Jesus. The Society of Jesus emerged out of his life and work. The founding of the Society of Jesus was an incarnational embodiment of the life of Ignatius. In a similar manner, though I am not claiming the global reach or impact of the Society of Jesus, my ministry has been most fruitful in staying on the journey with God and the Spirit.

PART IV

The Feast: Re-Forming Ignatian Spirituality

When he was at the table with them, he took bread, blessed and broke it, and gave it to them. Then their eyes were opened, and they recognized him. — Luke 24:30-31a.

SIX

Anticipation of The Feast

The characteristics of *The Autobiography* I listed in Part II have been very helpful, even foundational, but also insufficient for my spiritual life. The absence of other, necessary characteristics in *The Autobiography* will be the focus of Part IV, as I name the challenges of *The Spiritual Exercises* that this former Jesuit and former Roman Catholic has had to wrestle with and re-form.

The most significant missing characteristic in both *The Autobiography* and *The Spiritual Exercises* is a spirit of celebration and feast grounded in restoration of life to wholeness. The missing characteristic in my relationship with my Jesuit superiors was their lack of concern for the restoration of my life. My submission, my obedience to my superiors, was their central narrative. My life-defining discernment question and spiritual narrative of questioning authority was already in play in utero, in my naming, in climbing the high altar, in a second grade First Holy Communion class, and in leaving the Society of Jesus.

A critical missing characteristic in the life and work of Ignatius is that of restoration of life to wholeness in body, mind, and spirit. Ignatius' emphasis was on penitential surrender and obedience leading to companionship with God in complete and total indifference to manner or condition of life. The life of Ignatius, and his spiritual exercises, yielded much fruit for many. Notwithstanding the fruit of Ignatius, we need to critically reflect on the contemporary relevance of all of his spiritual exercises and question their role for our spiritual health and our participation in the mission of God.

The spiritual wisdom of any of the spiritual fathers and mothers cannot stand apart from the renewing spirit and healing love of the Jesus in the Gospels.

In the Gospels, feast and celebration of the restoration of life is always central to one's surrender and obedience. At the celebration in Cana, Mary tells the servants, "Do as he tells you to do," and later on the cross Jesus surrenders his life due to his absolute trust in the love of the Father for his only son. Nowhere in the life and work of Ignatius do we encounter the spirit of Ireneaus' wisdom, "The glory of God is the human person fully alive." *The Feast* seeks to correct this deficit.

Despite early signs of my resistance to blind, passive obedience to authority, I entered one of the most obedience-focused orders in the Roman Catholic Church, the Society of Jesus. In March and April 1983, in the first year of my novitiate, I made *The Spiritual Exercises* at Isaac Jogues Retreat House in Cornwall, New York, along with my fellow Jesuit novices, under the direction of our Novice Master, Fr. Robert Cloney, SJ.

The language of Louis Puhl's translation of *The Spiritual Exercises* that we used for that thirty-day retreat seemed foreign to me even many years prior to my formal protestant theological education. I struggled not only with the language but also with the pattern and rhythm of *The Spiritual Exercises*. Throughout the retreat, I made every effort to live into the spirit of *The Spiritual Exercises*, but I found them and my Novice Master's instruction at odds with my inner spiritual disposition and the movement of the Spirit of God in my life. However, as a good Jesuit novice I did my best to dutifully follow *The Spiritual Exercises* and the direction of my Novice Master.

With time, the gap widened between my inner experience and the desires of my Jesuit superiors, and my resistance increased with my early protestant desire to follow the Spirit in my life. My superiors matched my resistance with their greater insistence on my compliance with Ignatius' spiritual exercises and rules. I remember sharing with my novice master an account of my mystical, Spirit-filled prayer experiences. My novice master attempted to correct me and redirect my prayer to *The Spiritual Exercises* without apparent balance with Ignatius, the mystic in *The Autobiography*. I continued to pray mystically, and less frequently shared with my novice-master director. While I followed the Spirit, I lost that early grounding and indoctrination into *The Spiritual Exercises* that might have made me a more inculturated Jesuit. I was marching to the tune of a different drummer, and it became increasingly evident in my inability to comply with the Society's expectation of my obedience.

In this way, spiritual freedom did not emerge through my desire or my will, but only as the result of my intimate encounters with Christ through feast. In the intersections of my life with Christ's journey, the glory of God has been revealed. In these intersections is the feast. Feast begets spiritual freedom. Spiritual freedom begets obedience. Obedience is never first, but rather flows from feast, feast in the forms of love, trust, and joy nurture spiritual freedom into obedience.

Jesus cried out, "My God, my God why have you forsaken me?" Jesus was able to surrender his life on the cross because of his love for his Father. Jesus' whole life and death were in perfect unity with the Father. The Father so loved the world that he gave his only Son. Jesus surrendered his life to the Father because he was in communion with his Father. Jesus' obedience to the Father's desires would not have been possible in the absence of trust, love, and feast. Episcopalians say, "Alleluia, Christ our Passover has been sacrificed for us. Therefore let us keep the feast." Due to Christ's death, I have been able to enter the intimacy of love through feast. I am obedient because I am loved and I love.

SEVEN

Re-Forming Ignatian Spirituality for Feast

Here I share the way I removed Roman Catholic theological principles that played a foundational role in *The Spiritual Exercises* but were not easily transferable to me and many contemporary Christians. Many editions of *The Spiritual Exercises* use contemporary language, but in my assessment, none of them address these theological challenges. Pierre Wolff offers the most flexible instruction for retreat masters. But the exercises still need significant alteration for my use.

THREE CHALLENGES OF THE SPIRITUAL EXERCISES

Ignatius advises readers that *The Spiritual Exercises* not be read, but rather experienced and prayed through. I encourage readers to survey the exercises in a variety of classical and contemporary editions to become familiar with their theology. Your reading will likely differ from mine and from the reading and experience of Ignatius. Readers ought to encounter these differences and make their own choices about whether to adopt *The Spiritual Exercises* in their whole, unaltered state. The result should be a selection of exercises that resonate with you.

The Spiritual Exercises Promote A Theology Of Mediation

Ignatius encourages retreatants to see Mary as the principle mediatrix to Jesus and God, rather than directly speaking to Jesus or God. Ignatius encourages retreatants to go to Mary to get to Jesus and to go to Jesus to get to

God. In the first week, Ignatius suggests the following prayer pattern to close every meditation: "The first colloquy will be with our Blessed Lady, that she may obtain grace for me from her Son and Lord for three favors ...."[1] In the second colloquy, Ignatius suggests a prayer to Christ, and only in the third colloquy does Ignatius encourage prayer to God, the Father.

The English and German Reformations offered the scriptures in the vernacular, so every person could pray and read the scriptures without mediation and interpretation by clergy. A central characteristic of protestant identity is an unmediated encounter with the divine. When protestants "make" *The Spiritual Exercises,* they have to skip over the many prayers and ways that Ignatius invites retreatants to mediated prayer.

In my own mystical prayer, mediated prayerful discourse is an interruption and disruption of the Spirit's movement. Mediation is central for Ignatius, like spontaneity is the guiding movement for my relationship with the triune God.

Ignatius Theologically Conflates Christ, Church and Hierarchy

In "The Rules of Thinking With the Church," Ignatius presents his ecclesiology: "We must put aside all judgment of our own, and keep the mind ever ready and prompt to obey in all things the true Spouse of Christ our Lord, our holy Mother, the hierarchical Church."[2]

Ignatius' Rules for Thinking with the Church set the tone for his and the Society of Jesus' understanding of obedience. The example Ignatius gives is that when a subject knows that a piece of paper is white in every aspect, when his superior says it is black, the subject must embrace the blackness with his whole mind, heart and soul. Ignatius' rules are also thoroughly consistent with Roman Catholic theology where Trinity, Holy Eucharist and the Church are treated as one.

Alternatively, protestants are obedient to God and do not conflate Christ with church. Ignatius' theological conflation of Christ, Church, and hierarchy is disorienting for protestants and Anglicans who experience Christ and church as related but apart.

When Jesuit religious speakers speak, they believe they are speaking on behalf of Christ. Indeed, people are invited to find the person of Christ in their superiors and hear their mission from their superiors as mission from

---

1. *The Spiritual Exercises,* 63.

2. Ibid., 353.

Christ and God. Notwithstanding the weaknesses of my religious superiors, even if they had been the most gifted men, I would not have been able to accept their assignments as the will of God.

Ignatius Promotes A *Culture Of Fear* Through His Theology Of Sin, Satan, Hell, And Penance In *The Spiritual Exercises*.

Over and over in the first week, Ignatius offers only one way to experience the love of God: through God's mercy and the avoidance of hell. The retreatant is encouraged in the first prelude "to see in imagination the length, breadth, and depth of hell." In the second prelude, "I should ask for what I desire. Here it will be to beg for a deep sense of the pain that the lost have to suffer, that if because of my faults I forget the love of the eternal Lord, at least the fear of these punishments will keep me from falling into sin."[3]

In the protestant traditions, there are innumerable entryways to God's mercy and love. The Anglican custom towards confession of sin is that all may, some should, and none must. The first week of *The Spiritual Exercises,* with its emphasis on life review in preparation for a general confession, does not provide space for any other means to experience the love of God. The emphasis of the first week is thoroughly aligned with the penitential experience of Ignatius in *The Autobiography.* Some retreatants may enter the retreat with the experience of personal joy. The only way I am able to enter the first week is to adapt *The Spiritual Exercises* by re-forming them.

In The Feast, I invite retreatants to look over their life, searching for the presence and love of God, and to then give God glory.

As a response to these three challenges, I have re-formed *The Spiritual Exercises* away from an emphasis on mediation, fear, and obedience to an emphasis on feast. Through feast, we are able to be spiritually free and obedient to God's mission, as inspired by the Spirit through a mutual discernment of spirits in community.

Through *The Spiritual Exercises,* the Jesuit is led to spiritual freedom so he can be perfectly obedient. The purpose of spiritual freedom for non-Jesuits is more likely to be about prophetic readiness to serve the urgent needs of God's world, and less likely to be about passive obedience to the church or one's religious superiors. The shift from a thirty-day retreat, with the desired

---

3. Ibid., 65.

end of obedience, to that of a feast leading to spiritual freedom, required that the Ignatian retreat be recast.

There is a dissonance between *The Autobiography* and *The Spiritual Exercises*. In *The Autobiography*, Ignatius offers an example of his unmediated encounter with God; his discernment of spirits in his life review leads him to the founding of the Society of Jesus. On the other hand, while the retreatant is given great autonomy, *The Spiritual Exercises* are still mediated and oriented towards surrender of one's will to another. The re-forming of Ignatian spirituality as feast restores the autonomy of Ignatius in *The Autobiography* to all, as we each follow an unmediated encounter with God, reflecting on the ways our journeys have been guided by the Spirit through our companionship with Jesus.

EIGHT

Re-Forming the Thirty-Day Retreat Without The Spiritual Exercises

I have re-formed the thirty-day retreat so that we are left to dwell with Christ as we deepen our communion with God. A Feast thirty-day retreat keeps much of what Ignatius proposes and suggests, but invites the retreatants, together with their spiritual guide, to constantly review, re-form, and improvise their spiritual exercises throughout the time of the retreat and beyond.

I recommend that retreatants take much of the spiritual wisdom that Ignatius offers. I particularly find his elegant outline of the Gospels: annunciation, nativity, hidden life, public ministry, passion, death, and resurrection to be without parallel. (See the Appendix.) The elements of prayer as engagement, the principle and foundation, the autobiographical life review, daily examen, rules for discernment of spirits, and the Suspice are to be used according to personal preference. Rather than completely discard *The Spiritual Exercises*, I encourage retreatants to refer to *The Spiritual Exercises* throughout the thirty-day retreat and if they find them helpful, to use them, and if not to ignore them and remain focused on the scriptures and suggested spiritual themes of the week. *The Spiritual Exercises* can be a resource but not as a dogmatic, literalist narrative that trumps the Spirit working in and through the pattern of God's grace as God's primary way of speaking with retreatants.

THE WISDOM OF IGNATIUS I HAVE KEPT

Elegant Scriptural Outline for the Thirty Days

Although the scripture organized by Ignatius is elegant and can be deeply moving, I encourage retreatants to listen for the texts the Spirit places on their hearts and pray over these texts first before any suggested by Ignatius. I have been constantly in awe of the way the Spirit places texts on our hearts. In this way, retreatants are constantly encouraged to make all four weeks their own, following the promptings of the Spirit.

Engage the Scriptures in Prayer to Encounter God, Jesus, and the Spirit

Our primary prayer language is the way we narrate those places where we consistently find God and God finds us. Often for artists it is their art, and for poets it is their poetry. To start with art and poetry and then move to prayer and other spiritual resources is very different than starting with prayer and moving into art and poetry. The difference lies in who initiates our inner movement. To begin with art and poetry is often to begin where God is already acting in our creative lives.

Ignatius offers retreatants a distinctive form of prayer that he names as meditation, where each person enters every scriptural text. It is a valuable thing to read and study scripture. Yet, Ignatius shows us the way to engage scripture in prayer so as to insert ourselves into the story. In this way we are no longer spectators to a historical story. We are no longer just concerned with learning the facts of the story. We are a part of the story. When the angel Gabriel speaks to Mary in the annunciation text, the angel is speaking to each of us and awaiting our responses. In our hearing and in our responding there is potential for spiritual movement and transformation.

As an example of this profound way of engaging scripture as prayer, I offer my thoughts as a spiritual guide to the second week of the elegant scriptural outline. This week begins with call. The first suggested meditation is the annunciation. The annunciation is a wonderful meditative way to begin the second week. In the annunciation text we learn from Mary how to receive a call from God — not just any call, but a call that Mary did not seek or desire. We hear Mary's response, "Be it done to me."[4] Mary is available to hear and generously respond to the call she receives. Full of grace, she receives the call. The annunciation text is followed by the visitation text where we hear

---

4. Luke 1:38, Douay-Rheims, 1899, American Edition.

the beautiful prayer of the Magnificat: "My soul magnifies the Lord." (Luke 1:46.) The Nativity text is also a part of the second week, first day meditations.

The spiritual movement of the first day of the second week is call, response, and birth. In this movement, we keep watch as Jesus is born, but we also learn to actively receive call, respond and give birth. On this first day of the second week, Ignatius introduces the retreatant to repetition. Ignatius encourages retreatants, with their spiritual director, to be attentive to their need to repeat certain texts in prayer. He notes that special attention ought to be given to where we experience understanding, consolation, or desolation. Too frequently, when we read and study the scriptures, we are too quick to move from one text to another. If we follow Ignatius' invitation, then in our prayer we are invited to linger with the angel, with Mary, and with all the texts to follow.

In everyday conversation, twenty-first century Americans say to a friend or a teacher, "Could you repeat that, please?" So too, Ignatius invites us to repeat in our prayer parts of the story. As we repeat our hearing and praying, we surrender ourselves to become more intimate with Christ. To surrender we must be open. We cannot open ourselves up alone. We need to ask God for assistance in opening ourselves up. Sometimes we need God to open us so we can feel God's presence. The purpose of repetition in both *The Spiritual Exercises* and The Feast is to open ourselves to God, especially in those places where we resist God's presence.

We yearn to feel God's presence. We yearn for God's presence not merely for ourselves alone. The result of placing ourselves in the story is an amplified understanding of the way of Christ. It is similar to the words of Pedro Arrupe, which I cherish, the words of his prayer of the apostolate: "Above all, give me that Sensus Christi about which St. Paul speaks: that I may feel with your feelings, with the sentiments of your heart."[5] To be clear, Arrupe prays not for the feelings of Jesus' heart for himself, but rather so he may participate in the healing of the world's broken hearts.

The Principle and Foundation

The single page that Ignatius wrote before week one, day one, has had an unusually powerful effect. This one page is the essential grounding and preamble to *The Spiritual Exercises*. Although Ignatius never uses the words

---

5. Pedro Arrupe, (1983). *In Him Alone Is Our Hope: Texts on The Heart of Christ*. (St. Louis: The Institute of Jesuit Sources, 1983), 61.

spiritual freedom, the Principle and Foundation sets forth the cornerstones of Ignatian spirituality, that is, indifference and availability. There are many translations of the Principle and Foundation. Because of its accessibility, I prefer the translation of David Fleming:[6]

> Our whole life is oriented on being with God.
> God's creation is given to us as gift to draw us closer to God.
> If any of these gifts become the center of our lives, they displace God.
> And hinder our movement towards God.
>
> In everyday life, we must hold ourselves in balance.
> Before all these created gifts insofar as we have choice.
> And are not bound by some obligation.
> *We should not fix our desires on health or sickness,*
> *Wealth or poverty, success or failure, a long life or a short one.*
> *For everything has the potential of calling forth in us*
> *A deeper response to our life in God.*
>
> *Our only desire and one choice should be this;*
> *I want and choose what better leads*
> *To God's deepening life within me.*

The Principle and Foundation sets forth indifference. It is easy to confuse Ignatius' emphasis on indifference and see it as a Buddhist detachment from things. Indifference may appear to be detachment, and it is in part. Ignatius wants us to detach not as a purifying end but as a means to be more available for companionship with God and follow Jesus wherever the Spirit leads us. Indifference opens us up to relationship with God on God's terms. Indifference represents our availability to see God in all things and everywhere, under any and all circumstances.

Without indifference, we are otherwise inclined to demand that God fit our narrow experience of how God ought to be with us. Our narrow experience of the presence of God often is when we are content, happy, peaceful, joyful and patient. We should not confuse the gifts of the Spirit outlined in 1

---

6. David Fleming, 1978 *The Spiritual Exercises of Saint Ignatius: A Literal Translation & A Contemporary Reading* (Saint Louis: The Institute of Jesuit Sources, 1978), 23.

Corinthians as essential to our indifference. God is also present when we lack the gifts of the Holy Spirit. God is present in the darkness, in the turbulence, and in all the complexities and disappointments of our lives.

Indifference leads to availability. God is at the center of our resistances and yet Ignatius calls us to be available to participate in God's mission. Yet if we prefer the light to the dark, the order to the turbulence, and the obedience to the disobedience, then we limit the ways and times we experience and are available to God. Without indifference and availability, we limit the ways we are willing to respond to God and so we live in our chosen prisons of spiritual isolation when God is right there before us, but we prefer not to see, as we are waiting for an experience that we associate more closely with the presence of God. Indifference and availability do not always lead us to mission in companionship with Christ. Sometimes indifference leads to avoidance of those parts of our life that need reform and re-forming to lead to a fuller experience of communion with God and restoration of life.

In spite of all my struggles with the Society of Jesus and the four challenges above, the Principle and Foundation has on many occasions opened me up in ways that I never would have imagined. The Principle and Foundation has invited me to live into God's grace often in unforseen ways, uncharted waters, places I have not desired, places I wanted to avoid, and places I wanted to withdraw from. The shockingly simple practice of the Principle and Foundation is one of the most challenging and freeing ways to live into communion with God and generous mission.

Autobiographical Life Review

In a Feast retreat, an autobiographical life review is a daily discernment practice as a means to savor the presence of God in our lives. In contrast, Ignatius recommends a life review only in the first week of *The Spiritual Exercises*. The emphasis of his life review is penitential — to account for those times that we failed to recognize the presence of God. It is an exercise to search for those times we were sinful.

The life review takes two forms. The purpose of the traditional life review in *The Spiritual Exercises* is to recall those times of personal sin so we can experience the mercy of God. In The Feast, the life review is simply to celebrate the many ways God has blessed us. In recalling one's whole life history we can also begin to name a life-defining discernment question.

Yet resolution is never an ending, but rather an opening into a new and expanded wholeness with God. Our life canvas is always an unfinished piece of art.

The Daily Examen — The Practices

I have included in The Appendix, the New York Province Society of Jesus' version of the examen. Beginning in 1982, two times each day I reflected on my daily encounter with God. Initially I followed the prescribed process and it helped lead me through a uniform set of questions whose purpose was to assist me in recognition and acknowledgement of God's presence and absence in my life. Over the years the examen become less about scheduled times in my day and following prescribed questions.

The examen has now become like my breathing, an almost effortless review of my daily life experiences, drawing me into closer proximity with God or more aware of my distance from God's presence. It is my inward spiritual GPS and reset button that consistently reorients me towards the Light of Christ and wholeness of life. Even in the midst of re-forming Ignatian spirituality, the examen has led to the spiritual experience of my finding God in all things. The presence of God is now infused in every moment of my life. Increasingly I was able to point to God's presence in my life not only in times of prayer but also in the central parts of my ordinary life.

The Suspice

The words of the "Take, Lord, Receive" prayer of Ignatius echo the Principle and Foundation:

Take, Lord, and receive all my liberty, my memory, my understanding, and my entire will, all that I have and possess. Thou hast given all to me. To Thee, O Lord, I return it. All is Thine, dispose of it wholly according to Thy will. Give me Thy love and Thy grace, for this is sufficient for me.

Ignatius' prayer is offered in the spirit of Chapter 21 of John's Gospel,[7] and opens us to go to places we may not want to go, but where the Spirit leads us into mission.

---

7. E.g., "Very truly, I tell you, when you were younger, you used to fasten your own belt and to go wherever you wished. But when you grow old, you will stretch out your hands, and someone else will fasten a belt around you and take you where you do not wish to go." John 21:19.

NINE

Preparing for The Feast

My thirty-day retreat in 1983 was preceded by a week of slowly shifting the pattern of what had become my life. The entire novitiate formation program prepares the novice for the thirty-day retreat. In preparation for the retreat, the novice's schedule is modified to make space for this change in daily routine. Similarly at the end of the thirty-day retreat, the novice is given a significant amount of time to integrate his retreat experience before returning to his daily order. Very few people are in a position to dedicate six consecutive weeks to a time of extended retreat.

Accommodations can and should be made to people's schedules today, without losing the benefits of paying deep attention to the life of Christ. I have found in working with retreatants that a posture of flexibility can provide very meaningful experiences of the Spirit.

This re-forming of the time element is critical. With the centuries-long popularity of adapting *The Spiritual Exercises* for lay people, there is a tendency to think that one can only find the graces of retreat in the traditional manner. Simply replicating the number of days, or the practice of the exercises, or even the life of Ignatius will not create a relationship with God. It is relationship with God that was always the intention of Ignatius in his exercises and so too for us. The relationship is both within and outside of the thirty days.

It is important to note that the language of "week" for Ignatius of Loyola is a spiritual time, not an actual seven days. This kairos time has been lost to some leaders of Ignatian spirituality and has led to much less feasting. From this point forward, because of the value of kairos time, I will no longer refer to "a thirty-day retreat" and will rather use the language of a "long retreat." Indeed, many Jesuits refer to the thirty-day retreat as the long retreat.

A FEAST LONG RETREAT BEGINS WITH RELATIONSHIP

Unfortunately, many Jesuit retreat centers offer *The Spiritual Exercises* to retreatants without any prior relationship between spiritual director and retreatant. Ignatius strongly urged the retreat master to keep generous space between the retreatant, God, and the Spirit, working through prayer. Ignatius' counsel on distance is wise, but when *The Spiritual Exercises* is made between retreatants who have written a few autobiographical essays and have had a couple of conversations with their spiritual director, as is often the case in many offerings of the thirty-day retreat, the retreat has very different quality. Even when some pre-retreat work has been completed, the retreatant's relationship with the retreat center director does not match the experience of a Jesuit in formation.

When Jesuits make *The Spiritual Exercises* as part of their formation in the first year of the novitiate, it is expected that each man has made at least one eight-day retreat, has a daily practice of one hour of prayer coupled with the examen, and frequently meets with a spiritual director. For the rest of us to make the most of a long retreat, it is also necessary to commit to spiritual practices before the long retreat.

During this preparation time, it is essential for the prospective retreatant to participate in regular spiritual guidance for a period of at least one year, as well as active daily commitment to prayer, the examen, discernment of spirits, and engagement with the practice of indifference and availability. I find it preferable to be the spiritual guide of those who wish to do the thirty-day retreat for at least six to twelve months prior, to yield the greatest benefit of a Feast retreat. The re-forming nature of the Feast long retreat anticipates an ongoing relationship between the retreatant and spiritual guide. The spiritual guide should not be meeting the retreatant for the first time on the morning of the first day.

Ignatius knew that getting away for thirty days is a privilege not all are able to afford, obtain, or access. As a former Jesuit and now an Episcopal priest, when I have been asked to serve as spiritual guide, I too meet retreatants where they are. Together we craft the Feast long retreat experience as they desire within their time and financial resources.

MOVEMENTS WITHIN THE FEAST LONG RETREAT

Building on the relationship between retreatant and spiritual guide, I now offer what has come to be a framework of movements within the days of the Feast long retreat.

Before The Retreat

On the first day of the thirty-day retreat, I offer time for retreatants to arrive and settle into new surroundings, then take retreatants out for a celebratory dinner. I begin with a celebratory dinner because the way I offer the thirty days and *The Spiritual Exercises* is as a feast God has prepared for us. God has prepared a table for us to sit at and receive an overflowing abundance for all who come, even those who arrive unexpectedly. God's table also offers that which we never imagined to desire, but which we may discover through grace and patient waiting throughout the thirty days and after. Then we enter into the retreat at night, in the quiet of the evening, under the stars, and when possible near water.

In the first week, Ignatius does not suggest any scripture texts. Instead of a prescribed list of texts or exercises, I listen to the retreatants to determine from their stories the texts and exercises that might be most helpful. Frequently, retreatants will tell me they woke up with a text on their hearts. I typically acknowledge and affirm the text that has been placed on the retreatant's heart. I trust the Spirit working through their prayer and openness to God, unless I have reason to believe that some other spirit is at work.

Week One

In the first week, retreatants initiate an Autobiographical Life Review in the context of the love of God through an acknowledgement of blessings, and a recounting of times when God has been very close and times when God has seemed more distant. I have found that retreatants need very little assistance in being aware of their sins, faults, and weakness, but need far more assistance recognizing their blessings and intimacy with God. Whereas Ignatius begins with a confession of sin and complete dependence on God's mercy and love, I encourage retreatants to begin with their blessings as a constant indicator of God's presence in all experiences. With an awareness of their blessings and the confidence of God's love, I find retreatants are better able to reflect on those times when they have felt the absence of God. When and if the retreatant wants to make a confession, I follow Ignatius' suggested practice of encouraging the retreatant to find another priest other than the spiritual guide of the Feast long retreat.

The Spiritual Move from Week One to Week Two

In the midst of the life review, retreatants may find themselves open, raw, and vulnerable. During this period it is sometimes challenging to trust God's invitation to walk with God into the second week of the long retreat. Trust in these circumstances is often counter-intuitive.

To trust when we are vulnerable and raw is a different kind of trust. When and if this is the case, it is helpful to pray over indifference and availability through the Principle and Foundation in our own words. For example, "I prefer neither perfect trust nor imperfect trust, as my one desire is to be with Christ." Trusting God when we are vulnerable and raw requires our faith to lead us to self-abandonment until our hearts and minds are able to catch up with our relational journey. Throughout the Feast long retreat, the retreatants have to trust their spiritual guide, who encourages them to pray and to continue with all that is unresolved in their hearts as they patiently wait for God to act.

I have found that the first week, and in some sense the entire Feast long retreat, and our whole life, is found in the tension between our resistance and our surrender. In the absence of clarity, we tend to resist, but when we surrender through the practice of indifference and availability, then our spiritual freedom to trust increases. In this way, the spiritual life often is indeed counter-intuitive. Sometimes the mind leads us to this insight. Sometimes the heart leads us to this insight. Eventually we come to a union of our heart and mind. Wherever we find ourselves on the journey of faith, God calls us to follow. We have the choice to follow, resist, withdraw, or to trust in whatever condition we find ourselves.

Weeks Two to Four

Beginning with Week Two, Ignatius prescribes scripture texts and other prayer content with little room for adaptation. Despite this rigidity, Ignatius was flexible in the various ways the spiritual director could move from one scripture text to the next. Ignatius always encouraged the retreat master to listen to the Spirit for the readiness of the Jesuit retreatant to move from story to story in the Gospels. Even in The Feast long retreat, it is important to remember that the Gospel stories are best when savored until all the fruit has been yielded through prayer.

Week Two

Week two is a luxurious opportunity to deeply enter, follow and linger for hours with the life of Christ from annunciation, nativity, hidden life, and public ministry. With each Gospel story, I encourage retreatants to bring their own life stories as culled from their life review of week one, and to converse with the three divine persons. For Jesuits, Week Two is the time to make a choice of life, i.e., vocation. When I guide retreatants who are discerning a choice in their own life, I introduce the relevant exercises of Ignatius for their consideration and we work together to assess their value.

The Spiritual Move from Week Two to Week Three

I remember after Week Two, the mid-point in my long retreat, that there was a lull in conversation with my spiritual director. I have noticed the same thing with my Feast retreatants. Less time by the retreatants with the spiritual guide and more time in the thin space is a very good thing. Spiritual guides should not long for more conversation, but be constant in their presence and in their absence. Good spiritual guides stay out of the way, so the Spirit is more central.

In our contemporary culture, we are in a constant rush to get on to the next project. It is so easy for retreatants to listen to that voice in the mind that says, "Ah, half way through and soon we will be going home. Why would anybody stop all they are doing, go to a remote location and pray for thirty days? And, of what possible use is it to empty ourselves of our routines and patterns?" It is crucial for the spiritual guide to lead the Feast retreatants in staying attentive to the rhythm of the long retreat, as much more fruit awaits them. It is our human nature to be tempted to prematurely unwrap the gifts of the Feast long retreat. Staying present is a necessary self-offering of the retreatant to God.

Week Three

Week Three is the week of the passion and death of Christ. The entire focus of the week is being with Christ in his suffering leading to the cross. This week is often a difficult week for retreatants as well as Jesuits. There is a tendency to either extend the introspection of Week Two or rush to the fourth week, with little time spent in the third. Ignatius anticipated that not everybody would be prepared to move through Week Three.

In re-forming the long retreat as Feast, I have become particularly sensitive to the pain and suffering each retreatant is able to handle. And yet I do not suggest avoiding some time with these themes. When retreatants share that they simply cannot address the passion of Christ because of suffering in their own lives, it can be an indicator of what they may need to address in therapy outside of the long retreat. In some cases the days spent in life review open new awareness. Even while unresolved, these feelings can be savored and celebrated. If this is the case, the spiritual guide can gently move with the Feast retreatant toward Week Four.

Week Four

Week Four is the time to recognize how the resurrection of Jesus affects each retreatant in the world. The time is not to be spent simply gazing past the cross to the resurrection of Jesus, but for the retreatants to recognize their own movement from introspection through the resurrection with Christ, going forth into the world to participate in God's mission. Central to this week is the fulfillment of God's mission in Jesus and in each one of his followers. Just as the entire story of salvation changes due to resurrection, we too are changed. The exuberance of this week is to know the story and find our way into this message of abundant hope and love through our own ministry in the world. Without a strong emphasis on our participation in God's mission, Week Four, and in fact all of the Feast long retreat, can become stagnant and an example of the ultimate privatization of spirituality. The life-changing effect of the Feast long retreat through Week Four is that, like Mary, the disciples, and the apostles, we too are changed through our encounter with Christ.

I have found more than once the value of retreatants returning to their daily life and work as they begin Week Four before completing the Feast long retreat. To prayerfully reflect on the resurrection concurrent with their life and work necessarily places resurrection at the center of their life's work and practice.

Journey from Anxiety to Feast Before the Long Retreat

Even with the best preparation, there is always some anxiety. In my work with retreatants who have explored the prospect of a Feast long retreat, I have become aware of retreatants' anxiety(ies) in anticipation of their retreat. The anxiety is so great for some, they might even cancel their desired retreat.

Those who bring their anxiety into the retreat sometimes bring with them unreasonable demands of the retreat center and or God. These demands function as ways the retreatant expects to experience God and grace; otherwise the Feast retreat is considered a failure.

Those who enthusiastically look forward to the long retreat sometimes have not found affirmation from their family and friends. Anxiety arises not only in the retreatant but also among families, friends and work companions of the one who desires to do the long retreat. Some families and friends will ask the prospective retreatant why would anybody do a long retreat? Some retreatants will arrive to the Feast long retreat broken down by their families and friends, wondering if they missed something or questioning if they have been told everything they might reasonably expect to encounter.

Previously my experience with the thirty days as a Jesuit was very different than retreatants who are anxious. *The Spiritual Exercises* in the form of a thirty-day retreat is the centerpiece of the Jesuit novitiate and the novice's formation. Jesuit novices in my year and many other years have reported to me that *The Spiritual Exercises* were something that novices could not wait to do. In the desire to be a Jesuit is also a yearning to experience Ignatius of Loyola's spiritual exercises.

Anxiety is normal for all who plan for a Feast long retreat. Anxiety is also a good indicator to the spiritual guide that the experience for persons who are not Jesuits will be very different. The spiritual director manuals, as well as Ignatius' own notes through *The Spiritual Exercises,* including the form and manner, are far more consistent with the formation needs of Jesuits and far less helpful for everybody else.

There are many ways to enter the Feast long retreat. I offer one way that represents my theology, spirituality and mission. Ignatius has influenced me, but I do not rigidly follow *The Spiritual Exercises,* since in their original form they reflect his theology, spirituality and mission. I honor his discerning and praying spirit by being attentive to the Spirit of God working through me. I encourage my retreatants to do the same.

PART V

Feast Invitations and Responses

I will greatly rejoice in the Lord, my whole being shall exult in my God.
— Is. 61:10a.

Even before the publication of this book, I shared my experience of feast with many people. Many women and men have experienced The Feast in its short form of five- to eight-day retreats. As I noted in the Acknowledgements, three women experienced The Feast retreat in its long retreat form. I invited these women, Rosa and Deborah and Marilyn, to share their experiences of The Feast with you. Marilyn's account became the meditation on form and re-forming that opens this book. In this part, Deborah and Rosa recount their experiences of The Feast. In reading their reflections it is my hope that you will imagine more ways to participate in re-forming the Ignatian long retreat. The reflections are each very different, as each woman emphasizes different aspects of her long retreat.

While each reflection holds its own distinctive beauty, they also share the same spiritual guide, a life review, and Feast spiritual exercises as outlined in Part II of this book. Finally, it is my hope that by reading all of our Feast reflections that you will begin to imagine those aspects of The Feast where you are drawn into a deeper awareness of your relationship with God and begin to re-form your own received spiritual wisdom in ways that reflect your spiritual exercises.

TEN

My History with the Spiritual Exercises of St. Ignatius of Loyola

by Deborah Kempson-Thompson[8]

October 2014

On the first day of our spiritual journey we, the retreatants and director, drove through the golden hued Sierra autumn to bright blue Donner Lake beneath a twin sky. I walked alone and silent along the west shore of the lake. I thought of Lake Galilee — the anticipation and excitement of the newly called disciples walking with Jesus along that other shore.

Along the western shore of Donner Lake
Seaweed floated and banged against the shoreline
No, not seaweed,
Green but alien to lake waters
A branch, a broken piece of earth
Floating far from home

---

8. A lifelong Episcopalian, the Rev. Deborah Kempson-Thompson received her Masters of Divinity from the Church Divinity School of the Pacific in Berkeley, California. She is a priest in the Episcopal Diocese of Nevada. Deborah has been published previously, and prior to ordination she was a small business administration consultant and manager. Having a MA in English and teaching credentials in California and Florida, she taught for many years after leaving her first career as a media producer/director.

Neither waterborne nor shore-bound
Lapped in a circuit,
Now brushed against the sand
Now reclaimed by water
Alien, not integral—
No less dependent
On water and wind
Than it was before—
But lifeless.

I wanted more lively movement in my life. Like a ballerina in a body suit, I wanted to dance, fall, and rise in new ways, to let God be present to me anew — to levitate and fly in a more powerful way — jeté!

I stopped, breathed deeply, and silently exclaimed, avowed, and hoped, "I am open!" Then I joined the others to sit in silence at the shoreline, reflecting individually in unison.

My retreat became a journey of liberation fueled by impressions and insights that emerged as poems. The weeks filled day by day with vivid images of life and power. Putting myself in the scenes of Jesus' life — imagining the sights, smells, emotions — entwining my imagination with the life of Christ, I walked each day and sat outside at a picnic bench, journal at hand and relaxed in the presence of the Master, observing my surroundings with an open, fresh spirit. This was a novel pursuit for me as I tend to be inward and analytical.

The anxious wait for deep peace and contentment was about to be over.

Week One — Where Have I Embraced God? Where Have I resisted?

During the first week, I realized that all my life, I've wanted more or less — more love, peace, comfort, time; less worry, confusion, material encumbrance, stress. During the Thirty Days, I literally discovered a whole new world within and without through the dimension of my senses that enabled me to surrender to *God is Everywhere* — from intellectual knowledge and belief toward Presence.

Pay attention! adjured the Holy Spirit. No need to strive for a far off time of peace and manageable service in my life.

Recall to my heart, O Lord
those times in darkness and light,
strife and sorrow
joy and safety
illness and health
When you were present and
I heeded your call, comfort,
inspiration, and companionship.
Reveal to me where I have resisted you
That by insight I might find you there as well.

During this week. I come to understand a little more of St. Paul's reminder to the church in Corinth, *Already you are rich, already you are full.* That same satisfaction that I treasured alone with God, especially in crises, becomes available to me in the present moment wherever I find myself on retreat — in quiet joy, during support for times of regret, in anxiety, in laughter, in common tasks like cooking, and in Holy Communion.

Impressions
Bold blue and black of Steller's Jays,
Deep burnt sienna bark and dark green leaves
Knotty cedars making shadows longer and longer as time goes by
Piercing autumn breezes
Incessant click-click of squirrels chatting
    Rushing from tree to tree with one nutty find at time
Invalid rays of sunshine struggling through
    Thick, shaggy pine and cedar forest canopy
    Creating pools of tepid light
Pine needled ground
    Pungent when even slightly warmed
Brilliant yellow, heart-shaped aspen leaves
    Quivering in the wind
    Refusing to give up their hold upon mottled gray and white branches
Constant whooshes of traffic and the acrid odor of auto exhaust
Clanging-banging of road repair

Night made day by highway construction lights

Staging area made bright as a Friday night football stadium

Stolen sleep

Kitchen window glass crashing under

> Heavy bear paws

> Hungry for chocolate cake

Soothing thrum and motion of cushy rocking chair

Abrasive old sofas and stiff metal chairs

Motley décor and tasty meals

Sympathetic eyes and sage conversation

Rough tree bark, prickly pinecones

Cool polished wood of chapel pews

Powerful aroma of warm communion wine

Substantial heft of whole grain communion bread

> All these sensuous gifts of life, and more, become mine for the listening, watching, feeling, smelling, touching, and tasting — experiencing God in situ.

I step out of the chapel early in the week into a chill and shaded late afternoon. The labyrinth, only a stride away, is outlined in white paint on the asphalt driveway. I step onto its circuitous path ready "to get to the heart of the matter" — having no idea what my mind means by that phrase. Quietly, slowly I walk and turn and walk toward the center. The chilly breeze fights with my scarf for a place on my neck, my nostrils fill with thin clean air, my mind slips into mantra mode. I walk and turn and walk and wonder at the phrase weaving its way through my mind, "get to the heart of the matter."

Reaching the center — chin lifted, eyes closed, arms outstretched, breath coming deeply and unhurriedly — I stand still.

The light upon my closed eyelids grows surprisingly brighter and brighter. Peace fills my whole body, my mind empties, my heart swells. I am experiencing serenity for the first time. Serenity — freedom from all anxiety, confidence in God — becomes for me in that moment the heart of the matter. In that moment, I comprehend *now.* I glimpse *I am.*

A calm voice in the night calls at 4:19 a.m. — *Deborah?* A sleepy me opens the door to no one in the warmly lit hallway. Huh. The following day no caller in the night can be found to admit to the deed. Huh. What am I to think? Samuel comes to mind,

Speak, Lord, your servant hears.
Disabled, disenchanted humanity
Hear the voice of God
I AM — not a fallible parent.
I AM — not capriciousness
I AM — not betrayal
I AM — Love
I AM — Song
I AM — Play
I AM — Purpose
I AM — Mystery
I AM — Celebration
I AM — Everywhere!

Walking the asphalt path through a corridor of tall trees, I am illuminated by the weak sunshine but not warmed. Further along the path, I walk into shade. Oddly this darkness makes the greens, browns, reds, and blacks of the forested path more intense. Toward the end of the path, I pass a small row of cedar volunteers — upright, fresh, and skinny as teenagers. *Bless these beautiful little trees, O Lord, with robust life as they grow here into adulthood.* Farther on I enjoy the preening and prancing of the jays on the forest floor and their winging into high tree branches, scolding me as they go. I laugh. I don't feel like an invader. Turning to walk back, I pass the saplings again — smile their way, inhale the cool cedar scented air, then my whole body begins to fill up with beauty — I am plump with beauty. My goodness! One can *feel* beauty! I never knew. I am awed and made grateful by the ordinary.

Week Two — Imagine!
What ordinary sights and sounds and pains encompass Mary and Joseph, what surprises await Jesus in the Nativity — anxiety, relief, and adoration.

Newly Born in Bethlehem
A woman crouching
folds and unfolds upon herself
clutching her skirts above her knees

Wide eyes give way to closed,
opening and closing in waves
of moans, sighs, and howls.

A man, stooping,
splays rough hands
below the woman's knees.

Narrowed eyes give way to wide
oscillating in waves
of gasps, pants, and puffs.

A newborn, flying,
bounces bottom first
like a wood chip from a carpenter's awl
into a father's hands.

Wide eyes give way to narrowed
bawling in waves
of charity, hope, and faith.
Eternal life, wailing,
erupts from bloody embryonic fluid
a shooting star in the violet night,
crowned with vernix.

Newborn, Behold the World
Acrid fluids
sweat, blood, and urine

Bleating sheep and goats
slitty eyed and pointy faced

Mud and dung
pungent, slimy

Fresh hay and solid wood
sweet, prickly, hard

Human hands
tender, caressing

Human voices,
murmured reverence

Human tears
salty love

Human eyes
adoring one another.

Reflections: *I think most of us are more frightened and willful than we need to be.*

As human, beings we are small, but we are as essential and as important to God as a single drop of rain is necessary to an ocean.

"Knit your ministry to your heart," says my spiritual director. I think he means I must be led by the Lord in both my strengths and weaknesses.

He urges me to remember that "priesthood lies at the junction of death and resurrection." The cross and the empty tomb. I am to be aware, indifferent — preferring neither one over the other, perceiving that in both lie reality and balance. This is life in Christ Jesus.

I am reminded of a dream from long ago. The automobile I'm driving swerves into a woodsy lane so narrow it pinches. Suddenly my auto becomes a bicycle.

Freedom
Spinning through the trees
Sunlight and shade chasing me.
Leaving the path
Racing through the woods
Leaves slap my face.
"Beware," shouts the quarry, "lake ahead,

"Bikes don't float!"
This one will.
I plunge. I surface.

Reflection: *Surrender to freedom. Serenity and peace follow decision making in God's presence, conviction follows, too.*

Week Three — Control

The greatest of my temptations is control — I always want to know, to intervene, to tend, to prevent, to encourage, *to do something.*

Sometimes — often — well, most of the time — life affords me none of these. Christ Jesus himself must have felt so powerless, so frustrated when contemplating his death — leaving those he loved, sorrowing over their loss of him.

Mary, Mother of Jesus

How torn you must be in
this hushed moment after
crucifixion.
Your son is free at last from
pain and persecution.
But lost to you forever.
Oh, how you miss him.

I Will Sit with You

I will sit with you, Mary,
And weep.

Backs to the gaping sepulchral blackness,
Dampness sneaks across the rocks
To settle in our garments,
In our souls.
Our marrow collapses before
The forlorn onslaught of
The bleak invader.

We weep.

What of his bones?
Survivors of crucifixion
Now broken?
Now scattered?
His flesh,
Once plump with lively warmth,
Now ripped?
Now wrenched from a skeletal life,
By wild and hungry beasts?

We weep.

Bowing desultory heads and
Shoving useless hands
Between our knees,
We survey the
Funerary salves and spices
Gathered next our hems,
Useless,
Disabused of solace,
Pushed aside by discalced feet.

We weep.

Reflection: *Let me live the rest of my years in joy not sorrow when contemplating the loneliness and abandonment that is death.*

May I revel in creation — mind, body, spirit — all as one.

When I come to a Gethsemane decision of any kind, may I learn patience in feeling the agony of doubt and fear, those frequent companions of decision making. May I live with decision making as it runs its course until I reach my heart, until I reach the heart of the matter.

Week Four — It Is We Who Are Changed

It occurs to me that between the Resurrection and Ascension, Jesus goes on doing exactly the same things he's done throughout his ministry — teaching, healing, feeding, showing compassion. It is we who are changed by the Resurrection from fearful to bold, sorrowful to sanguine, from sheep to shepherds.

Resurrection
First, one
  Mary?
  Rabboni!

Then, Two
  Did not our hearts burn within us
    When he opened our eyes?

Then, three and four
  He is not here,
    He is risen.

Then, seven
  Taking charbroiled fish
    from the Master's hand.

Then, ten
  Peace be with you.
    The promise of the

Holy One is upon you.

Then, eleven
    Reach out, touch,
      believe.

Then, one again,
    an ass
      a fall
          falling scales from
               enlightened eyes

Now countless
    And I one of them.

In contemplating my life *vis a vis* the life Christ Jesus, I have found a new contentment, not complacency. Whether I stand at the edge of my heart or at its center, I find I am not afraid or restless anymore.

Contemplation
Blinking in radiance
I stand—
Quivering like an aspen leaf
To the harmonics of
All the angels and saints
Singing for me!

ELEVEN

Hosting Grace — the Gift of Incarnation

by Rosa Vera Lindahl[1]

For almost four years, I have been privileged to engage in a sustained conversation with Joe Duggan. One of the many things I have learned in that conversation is that each of us has a life-defining discernment question that shapes the arc of our story. Mine is this: Can I move out of the valley of the shadows of death to receive and claim the gift of resurrection in the entirety of my being — body, mind, and spirit?

This essay is intended to explore how the Ignatian retreat in the form of a feast, with Joe's guidance, helped me understand this question at the core of my existence, and how those thirty days marked the passage into a new kind of life that is only possible because I have accepted the gift. Some background is necessary for context, though what follows is not comprehensive. Rather, it focuses primarily on the aspect of my being I have most consistently ignored and most urgently needed the blessing of The Feast.

BEFORE THE BEGINNING

An enormous part of my life work has focused on dissociating myself from my incarnate self. I was born with a dislocated hip that went undiagnosed

---

1. Born and raised in Cali, Colombia, Rosa Vera Lindahl is an Episcopal priest. Rosa has served diverse faith communities, traditional and emerging, in Southeast Florida and Central Alabama, where she is Associate Rector at the Church of the Ascension. She farms, whispers to her chickens, is the wife of Sherod Mallow, and especially, is the profoundly grateful mother of Luz Maria Mallow.

until I was 18 months old and already walking. The damage of such a late diagnosis was significant. After the post-operative care following my first surgery was botched, I spent four years in a full-length, hip spica cast. More surgery followed, along with years and years of physical therapy and marginalization because of my difference as a young child with a problematic physicality that included leg braces and hideously ugly orthopedic shoes. I cannot remember a time as a child when I didn't experienced my body as a source of pain, exclusion, shame, limitation, and loss.

Several other issues with my body became manifest as I moved into adolescence: I became quite nearsighted and had to wear glasses. When I lost my baby teeth, my permanent teeth came in crooked and protrudent. To make matters worse, the roots of my front teeth were so short, that I could not benefit from orthodontics. In fact, the only option offered to me by orthodontists was to pull all my front upper teeth and replace them with a bridge. For a young girl entering adolescence, the options were devastating.

To make matters worse, weight management became a serious issue for me at about the same time, so, from adolescence on, I have constantly struggled to maintain a healthy weight. In contrast, both my brothers were and are tall, good looking and healthy. I took to saying that I was the lemon on the assembly line, and sought my escape in reading, and, I recognize now, self-medication through food.

The next way in which I became alienated from my body had to do with the first stirrings of desire, when I discovered Harlequin Romances, also in my early teens. The child of parents who were profoundly uneasy about issues of sexuality, I was scolded and derided when my mother discovered me reading "such trash". What I went on to learn about sexuality I learned furtively, and with a deep sense of shame, wrongness, and despair. Unattractive and alienated from my body, I watched with envy as my friends, one by one, got boyfriends, and I experienced myself as even more thoroughly marginalized from life.

I can look back on my years in high school and recognize how I quite regularly sabotaged myself in the one place where I resided fairly comfortably, namely in my mind. Too insecure, I avoided pushing myself when academics got tough, particularly when it came to math. That in turn limited my options when it was time to go to college and I landed in a small woman's college in Virginia, even more isolated and alone. In fact, the experience was so desolating that I became suicidal in a way that finally made it essential to go far deeper in search of meaning than I ever had before. Some of the relief

I found came from therapy. But it was the welcome I received in a small Episcopal church, the community that incarnated kindness and created a place for me at the heart of itself that began to bring me back from the place where I teetered next to a spiritual and emotional black hole. I also found a language — theology — that began to open spaces to find my way back into my body.

It was only then that I began to take the risks of embodiment — flirting, losing enough weight to consider I might be at least a little attractive. Those first attempts failed quite spectacularly. Each of the first two men I "fell for" very kindly and gently advised me that they were gay. I am still married to the third man I fell in love with. But our start was anything but auspicious. His first marriage had fallen apart, and all the complexity, entanglement, and brokenness of a failed marriage defined the start of mine. At 25, I was not free to marvel at my first kiss, to rejoice in a new experience of my embodiedness that was so thoroughly about playfulness and pleasure. Instead, I was beset by more guilt, more shame, more of a sense of my own worthlessness

It is no wonder then, that all through my adult life, I have had, at best, a deeply ambivalent and conflicted experience of my embodiment, including continuing to struggle with my weight. That ambivalence and conflict came to a serious crisis in 2011.

THE VALLEY OF THE SHADOW OF DEATH

On a sunny, gorgeous afternoon in June of 2011, my brothers, dad, and I drove up a mountain road in Panama, through the exuberance of a tropical rainforest. We stopped at a particularly lush area, next to a river that runs wild and fast down towards the Pacific Ocean. My mother was dead. Two days before, we had accompanied her remains to the crematorium, and it had taken every ounce of self-discipline not to let my mind go with her into what followed next. The woman who birthed me, nursed me, tended to me all those years when I was in a cast, who drove and sang with me each afternoon on our way to my physical therapy, had died. What I had feared the most — coming face to face with the finality of a corpse, and then cremated ashes — had come to pass. Now, my brother gently opened the urn and tipped it over.

The ashes danced and twirled in the sun as they scattered into the river. My mom, who had a playful spirit, who loved to dance, had spent years in a wheelchair, cancer taking even her playfulness away. I was stunned to realize that instead of facing a moment of utter devastation and loss, this was one final, joyful reminder of the essence of my mother; I will always be glad that the last I saw of her, she was dancing with sunlight. Death and fire returned her to us. Incarnation means this too.

I came back to the United States to resume my life, aware that for a long time, I had been ignoring some signs that all was not well with my own body including constant thirst and fatigue. Now, after ignoring those symptoms, I made an appointment to see my physician. The blood work she'd ordered for me to complete before coming in to see her told the story in stark terms. My blood sugar was over 300 — I was now diabetic. I had been locked in a death grip with my own health, using food to self-medicate and self-anesthetize. I had avoided getting the most basic care I needed for health. I had quite absolutely given up hope on my body — which is the same thing as saying I had given up on myself. I had been committing slow and certain suicide — another form of magical thinking — allowing myself to be extinguished without making anyone upset.

The numbers when I tested my blood sugar each day confronted me with the reality, the harsh reality, of my diabetes. I found it in myself to adopt a vegan food plan. I began to walk. Over time, I pushed a little bit at a time, till one day I realized I was walking six miles most nights. I began to feel better. I lost over 50 pounds and found a new source of strength I had never thought possible — my embodiment. It wasn't that I was born again; rather I began to walk out of the valley of the shadow of death.

THE WAY OF IGNACIO DE LOYOLA

It was through my work in ministry that the pieces leading to a thirty-day retreat began to come together. An ordained Episcopal priest, in 2010 I found myself in a highly conflicted parish ministry about a year before my mother's death. A few years earlier, I had begun doing Latino ministries, first in soccer fields and then in storefronts. In 2010, my husband and I launched what we called a regional ministry that brought together the large downtown parish where he was rector, the ministry I had started, and a seriously vulnerable parish of the Episcopal Church located close to where I was doing my ministry. It looked like a wonderful opportunity to pool resources and do exciting, cutting-edge ministry. Within five months, it had blown up in my face, and on Pentecost Sunday, I had found myself facing my vestry (congregational board of leaders) as many of them screamed at me in anger over a situation with a staff member. Though I did not yet really understand the centrality of physical health to ministry, I knew that to lead this community through such turbulence, I need to be as spiritually healthy and strong as possible, and I would not find that strength through isolation.

For a number of years, I had heard about the Ignatian path of spirituality from a group of women pastors I had befriended. Aware of my need to be silent, and place myself in the presence of God in a very intentional way, I found a Jesuit retreat house in Maryland that had space in an upcoming eight-day silent retreat. I received three graces in particular during that time. First, a friend had recommended I take a camera because I would be looking for "God in all things" and a camera would help in my looking and seeing. To this day, photography continues to be central in my explorations and ground-ing in the world as a sacrament.

Second, I was introduced to Ignatius' scripture-based prayer practices. The act of placing my life and myself in the stories of the Gospel in particular was simply stunning. One particular passage was almost like a bolt of lightening in its capacity to illuminate the limitations of the ways I had been serving as the pastor of a hurting community. It redefined my understanding of myself as a priest and almost completely changed the terms of my relationship with the congregation when I returned from the retreat.

Finally, my spiritual director for the retreat, a gentle, kind nun, encouraged me to spend as much time as possible out in the beautiful grounds of the retreat center, located on hundreds of acres on the Potomac. Afraid that if I didn't do fairly strenuous activity each day I would suffer from even worse insomnia than usual, each day I spent at least one and a half hours in the morning and again in the afternoon, exploring the forest surrounding the retreat center. I can still feel the sweat running down my back, the burning in my legs as I climbed fairly steep hills, the joy when I realized I had actually managed to walk two whole miles. Though I would not begin the spiritual discipline of regular walking for another eighteen months or so, it was both a spiritual and physical turning point in my life.

FROM DEATH INTO LIFE

That same year, Joe and I met at a church conference and continued to run into each other occasionally after that. We began a conversation that evolved as we engaged my ministry situation in greater and greater depth. I was in desperate need of a sounding board and of counsel as the destructive complexities of the ministry I was a part of became increasingly clear. I had experienced the loss of my mother and, the next year, experienced another loss, when my husband and I had had to place our special-needs daughter in an intermediate care facility after realizing her aggressive behavioral challenges were putting us at serious risk. Now, a third defining aspect of my life — my ministry — was crumbling in my hands, and, because I was in a ministry partnership with my husband, even my marriage was at risk.

Over an eighteen-month period, Joe and I spoke almost weekly, and I went to visit him and his wife for a few days in early 2013. The situation I was in was entangled, messy, and had serious implications for me personally, and for a whole community. In that period, much of what Joe helped me do was identify an ongoing pattern of magical thinking, constantly wanting to have things both ways — to be a rebellious contrarian *and* still be liked; to be faithful to my own sense of vocation *and* keep the support of others who had a different notion of what my ministry should look like. I wanted to be a friend *and* a pastor in ways that were confusing. In some regards, magical thinking was, and is, my death-dealing original sin.

On a chilly day, sitting at a small café in Reno, Nevada, Joe invited me to consider making a thirty-day retreat with his guidance. The situation with my ministry was escalating into crisis. On the other hand, I had been walking six miles most nights, and was as physically healthy and whole as I had ever been in my life. Finally, I had begun to find my way through the deepest darkness of the valley of the shadow of death without self-medicating or being tempted to give in to despair. But precisely because I was healthier and more self aware, I recognized the need for time to go deep in a way I had never gone deep — into the Gospel, into myself in body, mind and spirit. Powerful sources of resistance almost derailed my plan to make my thirty-day retreat on the shores of Lake Tahoe. I arrived with Joe at St. Nicholas Conference center in Tahoe City on September 30. The next day, I wrote,

> It was a long trip but thank goodness, there were no flight delays or bad weather. After dinner and grocery shopping in Reno, it was time to come to the Retreat Center. Jen, the priest who runs the Center, was waiting and said she had a surprise — she looked like the cat who swallowed the canary. I had time to unpack and then we went in her car through town and parked where there were obviously docks below us. It was really dark, really clear, really cold. With the help of a flashlight we went down rickety stairs, and out

on an even more rickety pier. At the end, quite far out in the water, there was some light.

When we got out all the way to the end, there were two women. One was Megan Anderson, a gentle, lovely young woman, recently ordained, who is also involved in church redevelopment projects of the Episcopal Church. I met her a couple of years ago and she now works at the cathedral in Sacramento. The other person was her mom. They had candles and chairs and little late-night snacks. We visited till it got too cold, and marveled at the ways paths cross and throw-away comments bring people together in unexpected ways; how in the end, we are all connected.

By this time it was almost midnight my time, and I was beyond exhausted. Still, I could not stop looking up at a night so clear you could see millions of stars and the gossamer cloud we call the Milky Way. It took my breath away. This morning, I enter the big silence.

That night I experienced infinity. Now, almost two years after I wrote those words, I look back on the big silence and realize it was a path. There are a set of quite stunning trails around Tahoe, and from the first day I was there, a routine began to emerge for me: I would rise early, make coffee and read the daily office of the Episcopal Church, spend about an hour reflecting on a particular scripture passage in the Ignatian style. After dressing and tidying up the small apartment I was allowed to use for my retreat, I would fix a simple bag lunch and head for the trails.

Most days, I walked anywhere between four and six hours. The most strenuous hike I took was on something called the Rubicon Trail. One section of Tahoe called Emerald Bay is simply stunning. The portion of the trail I followed began at Emerald Bay and ended about five miles away at a state park. Although it is described as an easy hike, and a lot of it is, there were areas more physically challenging than I had ever placed myself in before. About half-way through my hike, I came to a place where there had been a landslide. The only way through required me to inch along sideways, leaning against the mountain behind me, with a drop of hundreds of feet to a rocky edge of the lake beneath me. I stopped for a little while, and focused on deep breathing, determined to dwell in that in-between space, literally between a rock and water far beyond my depth.

While that hike is the most vivid in my mind, I can't remember any hikes I took that did not include some element of challenge, some need to push beyond what I thought was my capacity and endurance. Over and over, I also thought I had seen the most beautiful sight yet, experienced the deepest sense of connection to myself and the Earth which is my home, only to be drawn even further, even deeper into the mystery of absolute and infinite love — God in everything.

Spiritually and emotionally, I found the same experience in my daily prayer and reflection. The first week in the long retreat was a time to accept the depth and breadth of God's love for me as a beloved child. Dreams I had during that week, the look back on my life, the time to slow down after brutally difficult previous months in ministry, left me so raw and exposed emotionally, I still remember that it was like my entire being had been sandpapered. Each week that followed, each movement, continued to unfold in ways that were almost constantly surprising.

It seems to me that the "both-and" I found in the spaces around Lake Tahoe go to the heart of what it means to call myself a person of the resurrection. First, to receive the gift of resurrection meant going deeper than all my artifices, all my ploys for self-deception, so I finally hit what I realized was a bedrock of fear. Whether challenging myself physically or spiritually and emotionally, fear had always been the foundation upon which I had built my life. Breaking through that bedrock was like death itself and it was the only way to surrender myself to living waters that are like a deep, crystal-blue lake.

About half-way through my retreat, the sun shone bright one early afternoon as I walked along the Truckee, a beautiful mountain river, clear and cold. Unexpectedly, I was moved to kneel at the water's edge. I cupped my hand and dipped it in the water, leaned my head over and poured the water on myself. I did this three times, saying "I am baptized by the Father, and by the Son, and by the Holy Spirit." Sweating, gritty, hot and tired, I lived, in body, mind and spirit, what we claim about the waters of Baptism: In them we are buried with Christ in his death. By those waters we share in his resurrection. Through them, through their wildness and capacity to quench our thirst, clean our bodies, and carry us to new place, we are reborn by the Holy Spirit. That experience — that living into the fullness of my baptism — that was what I had come for when I had accepted Joe's invitation to The Feast.

APPENDIX

The Feast Resources
and Some Spiritual Exercises

Let us keep the feast. — Book of Common Prayer, The Breaking of the Bread

DAILY EXAMEN

The daily examination of conscience is introduced in the first week of The Exercises. Ignatius' emphasis in the examination of conscience is on personal sin. Of the five points offered by Ignatius, the final four relate to self-knowledge of sin, pardon from sin and resolve to amend our lives. The first point is to offer gratitude to God for "favors received." Ignatius says the purpose of the general examination of conscience is "to purify the soul and to aid us to improve our confessions."[2] Without my discovery of a more helpful version of the examination of conscience, I would have added this spiritual practice to Chapter 7, where I listed unhelpful Ignatian practices.

In my first days of Jesuit novitiate I was given an alternative version of the examination of conscience, developed in the early eighties by the Jesuits of the New York Province. This version, featured below, is less about personal sin and more about spiritual freedom through indifference.

Would You Like to Grow In Intimacy with God?

God becomes available to us through the lives of individuals who share their gifts, and the Source of their gifts, with others.

---

2. *The Spiritual Exercises*, #32, p.18.

Saint Ignatius Loyola received a gift from God that enriched his Christian life. The gift was a "method," a way to seek God and find God in all things and then gain the freedom to let God's will be done on earth. This "method" allowed Ignatius to discover the voice of God within his own heart and to experience a growth in familiarity with God's will. This "method" involved discovery and experience; one becomes attuned to God's suggestions and supports for action, growing intimate with God's prompting and purpose.

Through the steps below you can experience his "method" of growing in a sense of self and the source of self. You can grow more sensitive to your own spirit — its longings, its powers, its Source; you will develop an openness to receive the supports of God's efforts.

"Love consists in mutual sharing." (Spiritual Exercises of Saint Ignatius)

"Lord, lover of life, your imperishable Spirit is in all." (Wisdom)

1. Recall you are in the presence of God. *No matter where you are, hilltop or valley, country or city, in a crowd or alone, you are a creature in the midst of creation. The Creator Who called you forth is concerned for you. The Spirit of God, sent by Christ, will remind you that you are gifted to help bring creation to its fullness, to restore it to the Creator's way. Ask the Holy Spirit to let you look on all you see with love. "Love is patient, Love is kind, Love is not jealous or boastful, it is not arrogant or rude. Love does not insist on its own way…it does not rejoice at wrong but rejoices in the right … Love hopes in all things." (1 Cor)*

2. Give thanks to God for favors received. *Pause and spend a moment looking at this day's gifts. Be concrete. Recall the taste of jam on toast, the fragrance of a flower, the smile brought forth by a kind word, an act of patience that gave someone ease. Take stock of what you received and gave. Notice these clues that guide living.*

Now look at the more permanent gifts that allow your participation in this day. Recall your particular strengths in times of difficulty, your ability to hope in times of weakness, your sense of humor and your life of faith, your intelligence and health, your family and friends. God the Father gives these to you to draw you into the fullness of life. The Father sent the Son, Jesus, to assure us that God's kingdom is being established. Jesus sends the Holy Spirit to guide and sustain us as we receive and bring life to others.

Pause in thanksgiving.

3. Ask for awareness of the Holy Spirit's aid. *Before you explore the mystery of the human heart, ask to receive the Holy Spirit so that you can look upon your actions and motives with honesty and patience … "When the Spirit of truth comes he will bring you into all truth." (John 16:13) The Holy Spirit inspires you to see, with growing freedom the construction of your life story. The Spirit gives a freedom to look upon yourself without condemnation and without complacency and thus be open to growth. "Love hopes all things."*

4. Now, examine how you are living this day. *Recalling the events of your day, explore the context of your actions. Review the day, hour by hour, searching for the internal events of your life. Look through the hours to see your interaction with what was before you. Ask, what you were involved in and who you were with, and review your hopes and hesitations. Many situations will show that your heart was divided — wavering between helping and disregarding, scoffing and encouraging, listening and ignoring, rebuking and forgiving, a word and silence, neglecting and thanking. See the opportunities for growth in faith, hope and charity and how you responded. What moved you to act the way you did?*

Notice where you acted freely — picking a particular course of action from the possibilities you saw. See where you now sense you were swept along in freedom. This "method" is to give you habits of freedom. What habits helped or hindered you?

See where Christ entered your decisions and where you might have paused to receive God's influence. "Test yourselves," St. Paul urges, "to see whether you are living in faith; examine yourselves. Perhaps you do not realize that Christ Jesus is in you." (2 Cor.) God's influence comes through God's people, the Body of Christ. God's influence comes through scripture, the Word of God. Now, as you pray, God's Spirit will help you know Christ's presence and concern.

As you daily and prayerfully explore the mystery of your self in the midst of your actions you will grow more familiar with your Spirit. You will come to know the Lord is with you and with your Spirit. Christ will continually invite you to love your neighbor as yourself and strengthen you to do this.

5. Pray words of reconciliation and resolve. *The Word of God is very near to you, it is in your mouth and in your heart for your observance. See, today I set* *before you life and prosperity, death and disaster… Choose life," speaks the prophet (Deut 18). Now, having reviewed this day of your life, look upon yourself with compassion and see your need for God and try to realize God's manifestations of concern for you. Express sorrow for sin, the obscuring darkness that surrounds us all, and especially ask forgiveness for the times you resisted God's light today. Give thanks for grace, the enlightening presence of God and especially praise God for the times you responded in ways that allowed you to better see God's life. In these acts of sorrow and gratitude you grow in knowledge of God's gentle labor for you. "As clay is in the potter's hand, so are you in mine." (Jer. 18:6)*

A Final Reflection

Growth in friendship and intimacy needs time and constant attention. Thus, give 10-15 minutes daily to this examination.

Cover all five points daily with a freedom to linger more at one point than another, as the Spirit moves you.

Notice how you grow in appreciation for the variety of vocations…among the People of God.

Pray that all hear God's call and respond generously to their vocation. "Thy kingdom come, Thy will be done on earth."

The above New York Province Society of Jesus (in italics) version of the examination of conscience shaped the way I pray and talk about my spiritual autobiography. Twice daily for close to three decades I have reflected on my daily encounter with God. Initially I followed the above prescribed process and it helped lead me through a uniform set of questions whose purpose was to assist me in recognition and acknowledgement of God's presence and absence in my life.

Through repetition the examination of conscience became less about scheduled times in my day and less frequently followed prescribed questions. The examination of conscience became like my breathing and the lens to my daily life experiences that drew me into closer proximity to God and those experiences that impeded God's presence. The examination of conscience became my inward spiritual GPS that reoriented me towards the Light of Christ. This spiritual GPS facilitated the Ignatian spiritual experience of finding God in all things. The presence of God was infused in every moment of my life. Increasingly I was able to point to God's presence in my life.

I live one life in the presence of God. In this way the Ignatian prayer resonated with my spiritual formation during my college years when the De LaSalle Christian Brothers began every class with the words, "Let us remember that we are always in the presence of God" followed by "Live Jesus in our hearts forever." The Ignatian prayer built on the De LaSallian spiritual foundation as Jesus was not only in my heart but also a companion with whom I took every step.

IGNATIUS OF LOYOLA'S SCRIPTURE SELECTIONS

for the Long Retreat

(see Louis Puhl edition of *The Spiritual Exercises of Ignatius of Loyola*)

Week One — Call and Formation: Mercy and Love of God

The Annunciation, Luke 1:26-38 (#262, re Ignatius' points)

The Visitation, Luke 1:39-56 (#263)

Birth of Christ, Luke 2:1-14 (#264)

The Shepherds, Luke 2:8-20 (#265)

The Magi, Matt. 2:1-12 (#267)

The Presentation of the Child Jesus, Luke 2:22-38 (#268)

The Hidden Life, Luke 2:51-52 (#271)

Jesus Goes to The Temple, Luke 2:41-50 (#272)

Baptism of Christ – Matt. 3:13-17 (#273)

All the above scriptures have been take out of week two and placed into week one. Not included above are #266 — Circumcision; #269 — the flight into Egypt and #270 — the return from Egypt. Add these to your prayer and reflection if you wish. Also, choose to drop some accounts.

Week Two — Public Ministry

The Temptation of Christ, Luke 4:1-13 and Matt. 4:1-11 (#274)
The Vocation of The Apostles, Matt. 4, Mark 1, Luke 5, John 1 (#275)

The Marriage Feast in Cana, John 2:1-11 (#276)
The Sermon on The Mount, Matt. 5 (#278)
Christ Calms The Storm, Matt. 8:22-27 (#279)
Christ Walks Upon The Waters, Matt. 14:22-33 (#280)

The Apostles Are Sent To Preach (#281)
The Conversion of Magdalene (#282)
Christ Feeds Five Thousand Matt. 14:13-21 (#283)

The Transfiguration, Matt. 17:1-9 (#284)
The Raising of Lazarus, John 11:1-45 (#285)
The Supper at Bethany, Matt. 26:6-10 (#286)
Palm Sunday, Matt. 21: 1-17 (#287)
Jesus Preaches In The Temple, Luke 19:47-48 (#288)

Not included above are #277, Christ Casts The Sellers From the Temple. Add this account to your prayer and reflection if you wish. Also, choose to drop some accounts.

Week Three — Passion and Death

The Last Supper, Matt. 26:20-30 and John 13:1-30 (#289)
From The Last Supper To The Agony Inclusive, Matt. 26:30-46 and Mark 14:32-44 (#290)

From The Garden To The House of Annas Inclusive, Matt. 26:47-58; Luke 22:47-57 and Mark 14:44-54 and 66-68 (#291)

From the House of Annas To The House of Caiphas Inclusive, Matt. 26; Mark 14, Luke 22 and John 18 (#292)
From the House of Caiphas To The House of Pilate Inclusive, Matt. 27; Luke 23 and Mark 15 (#293)

From the House of Pilate To The House of Herod, Luke 23:6-11 (#294)

From the House of Herod to That of Pilate, Matt. 27; Luke 23; Mark 15 and John 19 (#295)

From the House of Pilate To The Cross Inclusive, John 19:13-22 (#296)

Jesus Dies Upon The Cross, John 19:23-37; Matt. 27:35-52, Mark 15:24-38 and Luke 23:34-46 (#297)

From the Cross to The Sepulcher Inclusive, Ibid. (#298)

Week Four — Resurrection

The Resurrection of Christ Our Lord, The First Apparition. Ignatius notes the following: "First Point: He appeared to the Virgin Mary. Though this is not mentioned explicitly in the Scripture it must be considered as stated when Scripture says that He appeared to many others. For Scripture supposes that we have understanding, as it is written, "Are you also without understanding?""

The Second Apparition, Mark 16:1-11 (#300)

The Third Apparition, Matt. 28 (#301)

The Fourth Apparition, Luke 24:9-12, 33-34 (#302)

The Fifth Apparition, Luke 24 (#303)

The Sixth Apparition, John 20:19-23 (#304)

The Seventh Apparition, John 20:24-29 (#305)

The Eighth Apparition, John 21:1-17 (#306)

The Ninth Apparition, Matt. 28:16-20 (#307)

The Tenth Apparition, 1 Cor. 15:6 (#308)

The Eleventh Apparition, 1 Cor. 15:7 (#309)

The Twelfth Apparition. Ignatius notes the following: "He appeared to Joseph Arimathea, as may be piously believed, and is read in the Lives of the Saints." (#310)

The Thirteenth Apparition, 1 Cor. 15:8 (#311)

The Ascension of Christ Our Lord, Acts 1:1-12 (#312)

A FIVE DAYS FEAST RETREAT

An Example Of Supportive Materials Offered
to Feast Retreatants

The Feast is where our life story intersects with God's story and where God's glory shines through us.

In the days ahead I invite you to journey with Jesus from the Annunciation to Christ's post resurrection mission.

In the beginning was the Word. In our story God's word is the beginning, middle, and end. God's Word becomes flesh in our lives every day.

Through prayer and discernment I am confident, that you will recognize, name, and savor the multiple ways that God's story and your story overlaps, intersects, and comes together in shared mission. With each scriptural story and prayer text I encourage you to be attentive to where you are in the story or what part of the story is about you, specifically, your intimacy with God or companionship with Jesus.

Savor even the slightest intersections between Christ' story and your story! As you read and pray over the story of Jesus from annunciation to post resurrection mission, be mindful of your annunciation, birth, hidden life of formation, public ministry, passion, death, resurrection and mission.

Ponder every celebratory aspect of Jesus' story and your story in your heart.

Day One: Welcome to "The Feast" of your life in God and God within you!

Evening Theme: Annunciation

Suggested Prayer Texts:
God is within us! (Jer. 31:31)
God is with us! (Matt. 1:23)
God is among us! (Matt. 18:20)
Hail full of grace! (Luke 1:26-56)

The Feast:
The Spirit of the Lord is upon you!
Savor the presence of God in your life.
Locate the presence of God in your body.
Welcome the presence of God in your body.
Bless God within you.
Record your blessings.
Express your gratitude to God.
Be still and know that God is with you.

Day Two

Our morning theme: Nativity — The Birth of Christ Our Lord

Suggested Prayer Texts:
Luke 2:1-20

The Feast:
Celebrate the birth of Christ.
Recall your birth.
How has Christ's birth shaped your life?
What do you know about your own birth?
Offer gratitude for your birth.

Our afternoon theme: Jesus' Hidden life

There are three lines of scripture that point to Jesus' hidden life and the years before his public ministry. In what ways has your hidden life formed your ministry?

Suggested Prayer Text:
Luke 2:40, 51-52

The Feast:
Contemplate Jesus' hidden life and the ways he might have been formed.
Recall your hidden life and times of formation.
Recall the people who had a role in your formation.
Offer gratitude for all who have contributed to your formation for ministry.
Acknowledge areas of your life that you seek further formation.

Day Three

Our Theme for the Day: Jesus' Public Ministry

Suggested Prayer Text(s):
John 2:1-11 Wedding at Cana
John 4:1-54 Samaritan Woman at the Well
John 6:1-14 Loaves and Fishes; please add your own favorite stories of Jesus' ministries

The Feast:
Contemplate Jesus' ministries.
Savor and record the characteristics of Jesus' ministry.
Recall the ways you have been privileged to minister.
Savor and record the characteristics of your ministry.
Celebrate the ways your ministry has helped made known Jesus' ministry.
Record the ways your ministry continues to be blessed by the example of Jesus.

Acknowledge those ways you want Jesus to help strengthen your ministry.

Day Four

Our morning theme is: Passion and death

Suggested Prayer Text(s):
Mark 14:12-25 Jesus' Passion and Death
John 13:1-20 Jesus washes feet of the disciples
John 19 Good Friday

The Feast:
Recall and savor with gratitude the Simon of Cyrenes, Veronicas, Marys and Johns who have stood by you in your hours of passion and death.
Where has God been in your losses?
When has God's resurrection been most real, palpable and compelling?

Our afternoon theme is: Resurrection

Our Suggested Prayer Text (s)
Mark 16:1-11
Matt. 28
Luke 24:9-12 and 33-34
Come and follow me and I will send you! (Matt. 4:19)

The Feast:
Savor the times when you like the women at the empty tomb were convinced that Jesus rose from the dead.

Theme in the evening: Contemplation on the Love of God

Ignatius of Loyola invited the retreat in the last days of the 30 days retreat to *ponder how much God our Lord has done for me, and how much God has given me of what God possesses, and finally, how much, as far as God can, the same Lord desires to give God's self. Then I will reflect upon myself, and consider with all reason and justice, what I ought to offer the Divine Majesty, that is, all I possess and myself with it.*

Prayer Text:

Take, Lord, and receive all my liberty, my memory, my understanding, and my entire will, all that I have and all that I possess. You have given all to me. To you, O Lord, I return it. All is yours, dispose of it wholly according to your will. Give me your love and your grace, for this is sufficient for me.

The Feast:

Savor God's many blessings including those recalled throughout this past week as well as blessings from all creation.

Day Five

Our theme is: Sent out by and in God's Love

Over the last few days, where have you witnessed and experienced renewal of your spirit, call, formation, passion, death, and resurrection that points you towards reinvigoration of your mission or towards a new mission?

Suggested Prayer Text(s):

Annunciation (Luke 1: 26-38)
Call of Peter and the first disciples (Luke 5:1-11)
Call of Abraham (Gen. 12:1-9)
Call of Jeremiah (Jer. 1:1-10)
Call of Isaiah (Is. 6:1-10)

The Feast:

Savor being sent by God to participate in God's mission.
Give thanks for God's story from Annunciation to Mission.
Give thanks for the ways that God calls you into mission

FEAST COMMENCEMENT

Readers may have expected a Feast Postlude and are surprised by a Feast Commencement. A postlude is an ending whereas commencement is a beginning. In many ways my writing this book is more a beginning than an end. Of course, I set out to write a book on re-forming Ignatian spirituality and for now and at this stage in my spiritual formation, I have completed my project. In the course of writing I wanted to say much more about spiritual freedom, but it was first necessary to tell my spiritual autobiographical story and the way I have been formed through the spiritual wisdom of Ignatius of Loyola, re-formed and opened up by the Spirit of God.

A few readers have said that they heard some anger towards the Society of Jesus as they read my book. These readers are right! Anger is an important part of my story, of my re-forming, and of The Feast. I readily admit that my Jesuit superiors' unwillingness to engage my personal struggles left me to make my decision to leave the Society of Jesus with a rushed discernment that left me angry. To tell the story I have told here without some anger would be to romanticize my spiritual autobiography.

My spiritual autobiographical story did not begin with anger nor does this portion of my story end in anger. Upon leaving the Society of Jesus, a wise Jesuit friend encouraged me to postpone any decision to leave the Roman Catholic Church until I could journey from anger to love. It took me fifteen years, from 1986 to 2001 before I was ready to leave the Roman Catholic Church out of a place of love and not anger. By making the journey from anger to love I now have a deep peace that has strengthened my faith, ministry and commitment to a broken and fallible church. I am grounded in the Spirit led choices I made back in 1986 and the full life I have lived since. During this critical discernment period from anger to love I learned more about Ignatius of Loyola's Principle and Foundation, indifference, availability and spiritual freedom than at any other time in my life.

It was during this extended period of time that The Feast and my re-forming approach to Ignatian spirituality began to take its deepest roots. The test of spiritual freedom for my Jesuit superiors was my perfect submission of my will to their authority. The test of spiritual freedom for me is a capacity to dwell in and engage through light and darkness, integration and anger, certitude and dissent, answers and questions, community and isolation. I have come to trust and seek out spiritual leaders who have the capacity to walk in turbulent as well as calm waters. In the last few years that I have been able to articulate feast I have been committed to be a spiritual guide and pastoral leader who walks with others in their honest expressions of anger and grief. In the absence of or resistance to any anger and grief by those I have the privilege to spiritually guide and lead, I hear the insightful echoes of Joan Hemenway, who said to me many years ago, "Joe that is a lovely story, but where is your story of struggle" and coming into your relationship with God and self? In the early part of this book I recalled this Joan Hemenway story about her invitation to tell my autobiography with an emphasis not only on love but also struggle. In this book I have spent quite a lot of time on re-forming through questions provoked by anger, in my next book, I will return to love, through a re-forming lens enabled by feast that leads me to glimpses of spiritual freedom.

My life-worn spiritual freedom, feast, and celebration came through the crucible of personal and institutional suffering. Leaving the Society of Jesus was the beginning of closing my innocent encounter with the Christian church and beginning a new journey where routine questioning, dissent and restoration of life are critical components of my spirituality and ministry. When these components are absent I begin a process of self and when necessary institutional re-forming.

It is my hope that *The Feast: Re-forming Ignatian Spirituality* opens up for you innumerable paths and choices of living into the radical call of the Spirit of God.

As I read history through the lens of my experience, Ignatius of Loyola left the world three very different ways to follow Christ into mission:

The person of *The Autobiography* ignores the advice and counsel of many counselors and advisors who cautioned him at various points along his pilgrimage way to Jerusalem. Ignatius of *The Autobiography* had no superior other than the Spirit of God.

The person of *The Spiritual Exercises* continues to learn from the Holy Spirit although is introduced to the importance of the hierarchical church through surrender and submission exercises.

The person of the Society of Jesus indifferently surrenders to the will of God made known through the hierarchical church and his religious superiors.

I have chosen a different path through re-forming Ignatian spirituality. I am deeply grateful for Ignatius' spiritual wisdom that led to my path. I cherish my spiritual history as a former Jesuit and the opportunity that I had to make *The Spiritual Exercises*. I am grateful for the many lifelong friendships I have with Jesuits who through their own style of re-form stretch the church into God's vision by staying as members of the Society of Jesus. At this point I am grateful for all the experiences I had as a Jesuit.

In *The Feast: Re-Forming Ignatian Spirituality* I do not seek to be your religious or spiritual superior nor do I desire for you to imitate me or even practice The Feast. Instead it has been my desire to offer you a prayerful means to participate in your own unmediated, radically honest, spiritual, autobiographical, and re-forming spiritual exercises and practices. I pray with you that the Spirit compels you to embark on your own spiritual pilgrimage that you take with abundant openness to be formed by the Spirit of God for participation in God's mission. May all your endings be beginnings as each time you discover new depths of self-understanding and falling in love with God over and over to passionately share in God's mission.

ANNOTATED BIBLIOGRAPHY

Primary Sources for The Feast

Ignatius. *A Pilgrim's Journey: The Autobiography of St. Ignatius of Loyola.* San Bernardino, CA: Renaissance Classics, 2012.

Puhl, Louis, trans. *The Spiritual Exercises of St. Ignatius.* Chicago: Loyola Press, 1951. (I include this very dated edition, as this was the edition I was given for my thirty days retreat in 1983 when I was a Jesuit Novice. This is also the edition with which I am the most familiar.)

Introductory Retreat Resources

Silf, Margaret. *Going on Retreat: A Beginner's Guide to the Christian Retreat.* Chicago: Loyola Press, 2002.

Guenther, Margaret and Jones, Alan. *Holy Listening: The Art of Spiritual Direction.* Boston: Cowley Publications, 1992.

Merton, Thomas. *Thomas Merton: Spiritual Direction and Meditation.* Collegeville, MN: Liturgical Press, 1960.

Spiritual Guides and The Texts that Influenced My Re-Forming for The Feast

Arrupe, Pedro. *In Him Alone Is Our Hope: Texts on The Heart of Christ*. St. Louis: The Institute of Jesuit Sources, 1983. (Pedro Arrupe, Jesuit Superior General of the Society of Jesus from 1965 to 1983, offers one of the most beautiful, comprehensive reflections on the Gospels in his chapter, "A Prayer to Jesus Christ Our Model." The chapter is an excerpt from a talk entitled "Our Way of Proceeding," that Father Arrupe gave in 1979. At every Feast retreat I share Father Arrupe's reflections with retreatants.)

Brackley, Dean. *The Call to Discernment in Troubled Times: New Perspectives on the Transformation Wisdom of Ignatius of Loyola*. New York: Crossroad Publishing, 2004.

De Mello, Anthony. *Seek God Everywhere: Reflections on The Spiritual Exercises of St. Ignatius*. New York: Doubleday, 2010.

English, John. *Spiritual Freedom: From an Experience of the Ignatian Exercises to the Art of Spiritual Guidance*. Chicago: Loyola Press, 1995.

John English, a now-deceased Jesuit and once a contemporary leader of *The Spiritual Exercises,* offers one of the few writings on spiritual freedom. I frequently refer to his second and third chapters, "The First Principle," and "Foundation and Freedom and Commitment." I also deeply value one of his final chapters, "Life Experienced As Grace History."

Fleming, David. What Is Ignatian Spirituality? Chicago: Loyola Press, 2008.

Fleming, a Jesuit, offers a short, straightforward and easy to read introduction to Ignatian spirituality. I have used this book for my Spiritual Autobiography Workshop I have done in a parish setting. I also give the book to those who are new to Ignatian spirituality as a way to introduce terms, language and concepts common to Ignatius of Loyola's writings.

Several Editions of *The Spiritual Exercises*

Fleming, David. *The Spiritual Exercises of Saint Ignatius: A Literal Translation & A Contemporary Reading.* Saint Louis: The Institute of Jesuit Sources, 1978.

Ganss, George. *The Spiritual Exercises of Saint Ignatius: A Translation and Commentary.* Chicago: Loyola University Press, 1992.

Wolff, Pierre. *The Spiritual Exercises of Saint Ignatius.* Liguori, MO: Triumph, 1997.

Wolff offers a wonderful contemporary translation and commentary on *The Spiritual Exercises.* Wolff's "Annotations" are valuable instructions for retreatant and retreat master.

Additional Resources for the Spirituality of Ignatius of Loyola

Haight, Roger. *Christian Spirituality for Seekers: Reflections on The Spiritual Exercises of Ignatius of Loyola.* Maryknoll, NY: Orbis Books, 2012.

Haight, a Jesuit, offers readers, especially those who are seekers, an opportunity to engage *The Spiritual Exercises.* Those readers who want to retain The Spiritual Exercises but also find a way to engage their current spiritual tradition may find this book a helpful resource.

Skehan, James. *Place Me With Your Son: Ignatian Spirituality in Everyday Life.* Washington, D.C.: Georgetown University Press, 1991.

Skehan, a Jesuit, offers a very helpful arrangement of *The Spiritual Exercises* to be experienced by retreatants over a period of twenty-four weeks following Ignatius of Loyola's Nineteenth Annotation retreat for those who are unable to make the four week long retreat.

Veltri, John. *Orientations: Volume 1 — A Collection Of Helps For Prayer.* Guelph, Ont.: Loyola House, 1979.

The book, *Orientations,* offers helpful short annotations on a number of scriptures to fit a variety of retreat purposes. Veltri's book would be a valuable resource to those who seek to craft their own retreats.

Wolff, Pierre. *Discernment: The Art of Choosing Well.* Liguori, MO: Triumph, 1993.

Former Jesuit and an Episcopal priest offer a contemporary entryway to Ignatius of Loyola's Rules for Discernment and making spirit directed decisions.

Other Resources for The Feast

Culbertson, Diana, ed. *Invisible Light: Poems About God.* New York: Columbia University Press, 2000.

In the introduction, it was written, "No one knows God or speaks of God apart from experience, and our experiences are all different — and all limited." The variety of experiences invites personalized spiritual exercises that match the spiritual life of every individual.

ABOUT THE AUTHOR

The Feast is not a journey from darkness to light or from spiritual struggle to permanent freedom. In *The Feast*, author Joseph Duggan challenges the religious authorities who refused to walk with him as companions through his most burning struggles, ambiguities and questions. *The Feast* celebrates the companionship of struggle with spiritual practices that leads all on their pilgrimage into mission.

Who is *The Feast* re-forming author and how has he been formed to offer a spirituality that prioritizes conversation with God and listening to the Spirit over all else?

Key experiences have formed Duggan's re-forming vision and spiritual practices.

Spirit in love: The Ignatian spirituality that Duggan challenges in *The Feast* is also one of the major sources for his fundamental spiritual formation that gave voice to this book. The most influential part of his spiritual formation was what Ignatius of Loyola called "The Principle and Foundation." Duggan's superiors used this principle to insist on his availability, his indifference to all desires, and to submit to his superiors' desires. The Principle and Foundation has become for Duggan a spiritual power analysis tool harnessed in his reading of the radical ecclesiology of Leonardo Boff with his tutor, the late Professor Richard Schaull, Visiting Professor of Princeton Theological Seminary, during the Spring 1987 term at General Theological Seminary in New York. Boff's book Church: Charism and Power, with Boff's radical abandon to criticize the church he loved, offered Duggan a way to integrate his passion for God and desire to reform the Christian church for a new century of mission. Although *The Feast* is primarily about the Society of

Jesus, Duggan continues his re-forming passions in The Episcopal Church where he now serves as a parish priest.

Post-ideological theology: From 1991 to 1993, he studied to be a New York diocesan priest at St. Joseph's Seminary in New York, a seminary rooted in traditional doctrine and passionately committed to the papacy. From 2003 to 2006, he studied at the Episcopal Divinity School, known as one of the most progressive liberal seminaries in the United States. He received his PhD in theology from the University of Manchester in England, one of the largest and most diverse secular universities in the United Kingdom. Through all these theological learning centers, Duggan experienced a multiplicity of ways to be faithful, broader than any one of these institutions' claims. His broad theological and spiritual formation substantially contributed to his freedom to radical re-forming, and continues to energize him to challenge rigid, hierarchical religious systems that drain life out of the Spirit's bold call to mission.

Voice: Duggan began his life with a stutter and a lifelong tremor. Learning to speak without stutter and withstanding the teasing of boyhood friends, Duggan developed a deep and sustained empathy to befriend the speechless and those who are ignored. His voice was further strengthened as an executive working for major professional service firms and now as a scholar who is leading a knowledge activism movement through Postcolonial Networks and Borderless Press.

The Feast is always beginning anew, and Duggan seeks conversation partners who want to form their Spirit in love without rigid ideological commitments that unnecessarily divide, and speak with voices that liberate unconditional love into a world yearning for healing and reconciliation.

Contact details for further information on Feast retreats:
www.thefeastpress.com

Made in the USA
San Bernardino, CA
01 September 2016